A Stash
of One's Own

Knitters on Loving, Living with, and Letting Go of Yarn

An anthology edited by

CLARA PARKES

ABRAMS PRESS, NEW YORK

Editor: Shawna Mullen
Production Manager: Kathleen Gaffney

Library of Congress Control Number: 2017956867

ISBN: 978-1-4197-3290-4
eISBN: 978-1-68335-162-7

Printed and bound in the United States
10 9 8 7 6 5 4 3 2 1

ABRAMS The Art of Books
195 Broadway, New York, NY 10007
abramsbooks.com

CONTENTS

"*Perhaps there is no beginning and end to yarn, just a constant heartbeat of energy, a long chain of shifting shapes, from lamb to landfill, that started with the Big Bang and won't end until the next Big Bang. All we have . . . is the here and now. The yarn in our hands and on our needles at this very moment: That's our slush.*"

—CLARA PARKES, "WHEN IT'S GONE, IT'S GONE"

FOREWORD

My father was a professional musician for his entire adult career. He played oboe and English horn in an orchestra, and that meant he was always making reeds. For this, he had a room filled with tools with names like *mandrels* and *ballots* and *plaques* and *staples*, along with a well-worn cutting block, spools of thread in rich, shiny colors, and a little blob of beeswax. It was like Santa's workshop, if Santa were a woodwind player.

I grew up understanding the importance of tools and supplies to a creative person.

Yarn is the reed with which we knitters make music. We, too, have our rooms filled with tools that help us carry on our craft—things with names like *swifts* and *ball-winders* and *DPNs* and *circular needles* and *yarn bowls*. Collectively, they make up what we call our *stash*.

The specific tools may vary, but the room will always have yarn. Yarn is as essential to us as paint is to the artist, flour to the baker, soil to the gardener. We can improvise on most of the tools, tying string into a stitch marker, sanding down a bamboo chopstick in a pinch. But without yarn, our hands are idle.

As many kinds of yarn exist as there are people on earth. Each has a distinct structure and texture and behavior and ideal use. With so many options, and so many directions dictated by each choice, we require a healthy supply of materials in order to do our work.

A formal definition of *healthy* I cannot provide. It differs for each person. Most knitters dwell somewhere between "Gosh, I love my yarn" and "Am I a hoarder?"

We stash so that we can start a project at 2:00 AM if so inclined, but the relationship between stitcher and yarn goes far beyond simply being prepared. A yarn stash is a declaration of self-esteem. It is Virginia Woolf's "room of one's own," a significant financial stake in the ground that says, "My passion is worthwhile."

Asking a knitter what he or she plans on doing with the yarn he or she just bought is like asking a squirrel what it plans on doing with that nut it just buried under a pile of leaves. Obviously we plan on using it. Now? Later? For what? How can we know? Our main priority is simply to get that yarn safely back home and stored away in our stash. We'll know when we need it.

I once asked readers in a poll, "Without moving from where you are, can you see any yarn?" While 50 percent of the respondents said no, it's worth noting that 50 percent said yes. Which means that half of the world's knitters could, at any moment, toss you a skein of yarn without putting on their shoes.

Could you say the same thing about golfers or woodworkers or people who go spelunking on weekends? Without moving from where they are seated, how many of *them* could see golf clubs, or lathes, or whatever it is spelunkers use?

But yarn is far more than the sum of its parts, more than just a means to an end. Yarn holds hope and energy and history; it is a declaration, a question, an obsession, and a love story.

This book is a carefully selected collection of stories, statistics, tips, and manifestos on the subject of stash—specifically (but not always), the knitter's reputation for acquiring large quantities of yarn and storing them away for future use. The writers celebrate the meaning we attribute to yarn, the stories we let it keep, and the place it holds in our homes and in our lives.

The pieces in this collection cover the comical to the earnest, the lighthearted to the deeply philosophical, in a celebration of the *how*, *why*, *when*, and *what* we've accumulated (and let go of) over the years. They open our eyes to what *stash* means to each of us, both individually and collectively.

You'll find a full spectrum of voices, including knitwear designers and publishers, dyers and yarn store owners, along with a sheep farmer, an illustrator, a romance novelist, a handspinner, a Fulbright scholar, and a licensed clinical social worker to help us answer that common nagging fear: *Do I have a problem?* We hear from a knitting humorist, a PhD-wielding feminist publisher, the daughter of a shepherd, a globetrotting textile artist based in London, and a globetrotting designer currently based in western Massachusetts who may very well have moved again by the time you read this.

As varied as the voices in this collection are, they all have one fundamental thing in common: With the exception of our sheep farmer, Eugene, who gets a pass because he grows the fibers that make our world go 'round, every person in here knits. A lot. Which means that they coexist with a strong and distinct notion of stash every single day.

If you are a knitter who struggles to explain to others why your yarn stash means what it does to you, why it deserves so much more than a dismissive eyeroll, this book can be a start.

If you struggle not, if you love your stash and tend to it daily, let this book be your celebration.

And if you are a stash-aware nonknitter who wants to understand why your beloved relates to yarn the way he or she does, why that guest room simply *must* be turned into the stash room, read on.

All stitchers, you don't need me to tell you what our stashes mean. You live it. I'm preaching to the choir. In fact, this book *is* the choir, each voice singing loud and proud.

—Clara Parkes

INHERITING FROM ELIZABETH ZIMMERMANN
BY MEG SWANSEN

I am the youngest of Arnold and Elizabeth Zimmermann's three children. One evening when I was about seven, my mother divided a large sheet of paper into three vertical columns; she wrote one of our names at the top of each column. The paper was then passed around to each of us in turn, and we were to write down—one item at a time—whatever family artifacts we wished to inherit. Being so young, it didn't occur to me to put down the Things of Great Value that belonged to my family (as my brother and sister were doing). My very first choice was the dictionary. It was a grand dictionary—too large for me to lift—and it lived on its own lectern in the living room. The words *look it up* were frequently spoken at our house.

My choice was not based on a forward flash of intuition that my future as a teacher, writer, and publisher would be so entwined with words. Rather, with both my parents being multilingual, words were important, and the dictionary was revered. Like most families, we had our own invented words, and even an entire "cat language" we spoke to our cats (this having been acquired by my mother from her father).

Besides the dictionary, I inherited a tome of knowledge directly from my mother. We wrote each other silly letters in our made-up language and characters. Through her, I have memorized countless poems (both proper and inane). We also shared a passion for knitting, which gradually evolved from Elizabeth Zimmermann, Ltd., into Schoolhouse Press, a business that the two of us operated together with my husband, Chris—and which today is run by our son, Cully, and his wife, Michelle.

My mother taught me how to knit when I was about four. We

lived in New Hope, Pennsylvania. My memory of it is quite vivid: We were on the back porch overlooking the Delaware River, and I sat on her lap. She had her arms around me, guiding my hands through the moves. I was pleased and proud, and I knitted sporadically over the next decade. Being first-generation Americans, we had no relatives in the United States, so we sent and received Christmas presents to and from various family members in Germany and the United Kingdom. The first actual "project" I can remember was a scarf I knitted for my auntie Pete when I was about six or seven, back and forth in garter stitch—but with a series of short rows around the back of the neck to form a horseshoe curve. I had no idea what I was doing; I just followed my mother's verbal instructions. (Barbara G. Walker had not yet invented "Short Rows and Wrapping.")

During the decades with my mum, I inherited tips, tricks, ideas, and innovations through our knitting failures and triumphs. As I got older, we occasionally disagreed on a technique—like her idea to knit both strands together when joining in a new skein. Aargh! No. Leave two tails and darn them in later. Actually, that may have been when I taught myself to spit-splice.

I also absorbed Elizabeth's philosophical attitude toward knitting and life, which resonates through all her books: You are the boss of your knitting and can do what you like; there is no "wrong" in knitting as long as you are pleased with the results. In her first book, *Knitting Without Tears*, she wrote, "Now comes what I perhaps inflatedly call my philosophy of knitting. Like many philosophies, it is hard to express in a few words. Its main tenets are enjoyment and satisfaction, accompanied by thrift, inventiveness, an appearance of industry, and, above all, resourcefulness."

When you are obsessed by wool and knitting for as long as my mother was, you are bound to accumulate an impressive stash; not only masses of wool and needles, but books, tools, and other accoutrements of knitting. Included in her cache were swatches, fragments of knitting, abandoned projects, a sweater body with no sleeves, a single sleeve with no body, and even some unidentifiable artifacts still on their needles, for which there was no explanation. All these items were stashed throughout a vast collection of knitting bags, baskets, drawers, shelves, boxes, and bins.

Of equal (or perhaps more) importance are Elizabeth's journals, which contain notes, directions, charts, and sketches; some are complete, but many are just a shell of an idea, like a few bones of a skeleton. Can a knitting archaeologist build an entire garment from these sketchy clues? Some of the journals are overflowing with extra pages paper-clipped or held in by rubber bands. We also found stacks of loose papers: typed or handwritten pages, charts on graph paper, drawings, or hieroglyphic directions on the backs of envelopes or on hotel notepads. A knitting journal can be a fascinating chronicle of a knitter's life, where ideas, observations, failed attempts, and successful garments are all recorded unexpurgated; it becomes a stash of knowledge and a reflection of the author's creative mind.

One of my favorite finds is Fune Feat, her design for garter-stitch slippers. The idea was sketched and notated on a small memo pad from my father's office. As I knitted what may have been the very first pair of these slippers (I never saw this concept realized by Elizabeth),

A knitting journal can be a fascinating chronicle of a knitter's life, where ideas, observations, failed attempts, and successful garments are all recorded unexpurgated; it becomes a stash of knowledge and a reflection of the author's creative mind.

I didn't understand all the short rows across the middle of the foot until I was finished. Ah yes; to keep the sides from flopping out. It is a brilliant bit of knitted sculpture.

Elizabeth's archive is extensive. We are still unearthing things that, upon reading and/or comprehending what she was driving at, bring her back into the present day. Along with everything mentioned above, there are stacks of scrapbooks, plus correspondence with Barbara G. Walker, Kaffe Fassett, Gladys Thompson, and other designers and authors, many of whom Elizabeth both inspired and supported as they made their own way in this business. We have come upon a slew of drafts and published manuscripts, letters to and from publishers, notebooks of ideas, plus several accountants' ledgers filled with the minutiae of Elizabeth's early mail-order business records. I may even still have the thousands of file cards we kept, one for each of our customers, with every order recorded on the card as it was shipped.

Several scholars have spent time with this material over the past ten years. In 2006, Molly Greenfield, a graduate student in textiles at the University of Wisconsin–Madison, curated an exhibit of some of the archive as part of her thesis work. The exhibit, titled *New School Knitting: The Influence of Elizabeth Zimmermann and Schoolhouse Press*, was well executed, and I spoke at the filled-to-capacity opening event. In 2009, Kathryn Parks, an undergraduate student in history at the University of Wisconsin–Eau Claire, and her professor Colleen McFarland visited Schoolhouse Press and spent time examining sweaters and documents as they researched for their in-depth article in *Wisconsin Magazine of History*, Winter 2011/2012, with a photo of Elizabeth on the cover: *Stitch by Stitch: The Life and Legacy of Elizabeth Zimmermann*. The Wisconsin Historical Society was stunned by the onslaught of knitters ordering copies, and they quickly had to reprint that issue. Most recently, Lily Marsh spent several weeks over two summers with Elizabeth's works as she completed her dissertation at Purdue University. Other scholars have expressed interest in bringing the archive material to light. Though we do not know its eventual destiny, we are exploring ideas to make at least some of the archive accessible to knitters.

Elizabeth Zimmermann's remarkably unique approach to knitting was not inherited by me alone. It was delivered to innumerable knitters over many decades—both in person and in written form—through her frequent workshops, many knitting books, TV programs, and videos, as well as her semiannual publications, *Newsletter* and *Wool Gathering*. Elizabeth's "family" and "heirs" include all who read and are swayed by her words to this day.

When I was a kid, my mother's dear friend and knitting buddy was our neighbor Ruth. Our fenced backyards were adjacent. Since the two of them visited each other so frequently, my father and Ruth's husband, Frederick, teamed up to build a stile over the fence, which enabled Ruth and Elizabeth to zip back and forth with ease.

Decades later, when Ruth died, Elizabeth lamented deeply. My mum later told me how she had wished for something of Ruth's to hold—a knitting needle, book, pen, thimble—something relatively mundane that Ruth had cherished. With Ruth's family in mourning, it was impossible to hint (much less ask outright) for some small memento and, sadly, none was ever forthcoming.

I remembered that conversation clearly when my mother died, and the following summer I sorted through scores of her small knitted garments, some items still on the needles, bits of ribbing, the start of a sock, a single mitten or glove, a test Moebius twist, a bit of I-cord, and numerous Aran swatches. From this assortment, I put one article into each of sixty-five new bags and tied them with wool. Then all the bags went into a large burlap wool sack, which I took to our Oft-Timers' Knitting Camp.

I told the campers my mother's story about Ruth and that I imagined many of them felt the same way about Elizabeth. Most of them had been coming annually since the early years (beginning in 1974) and were doted upon by my mother. Over the next few days, during Show-and-Tell, each knitter was asked to reach into the sack—with eyes closed—for a tangible remembrance of their friend and teacher. The campers were touched and delighted, many going so far as to frame their "inheritance."

The most treasured feature of my mother's stash is her collection of finished garments: prototypes of her designs for sweaters, shawls, coats, jackets, baby things, endless caps, socks, mittens, and blankets. Many of the articles are missing from the collection, as Elizabeth was generous about sending her knitted pieces to friends, and to family overseas. The things that remained in her stash are now merged with my own, and together they live in a cedar-lined room.

For many decades before, all sweaters lived in large wooden boxes made by my husband, Chris. They were airtight and lined with eastern red cedar. In 2006, when my son, Cully, designed a new office/warehouse building down the hill from my schoolhouse, I requested a Sweater Room. It is in the middle of the building, and the walls are covered with eastern red cedar shelves. This is a wonderful solution to the issue of stash storage and preservation. All of our finished garments are within easy reach, and we often turn to them for inspiration or for solutions to technical difficulties. Like my mother, I keep my current stash at home all around me, and once a design is finished and published, it goes into the Sweater Room.

Elizabeth's philosophy of openness and dissemination of information is one I continue, and because of this, some of her garments travel to and from our annual Knitting Camps for participants to examine and scrutinize for their innovation and ingenuity.

They are especially treasured because her knitted garments represent love. Indeed, although Elizabeth's works were designed and knitted as tangible representations of the explorations of a brilliantly creative mind, they still serve as comforting, warm, functional garments for those she loved. I can trace the growth of our children by the successively larger sweaters their grandmother knitted for them. Those same sweaters have been worn again by the great-grandchildren she never met.

Elizabeth Zimmermann's stash lives on: both the physical garments that I inherited and, more importantly and enduringly, her transformative ideas, which she has bequeathed to all knitters.

STASHERS: WHO THE HECK ARE WE?
A PEEK AT THE NUMBERS, LOOKING FOR ANSWERS
BY LELA NARGI

Wherever there are knitters, there are, inevitably, stashers—those of us who accumulate great numbers of balls of fiber for reasons ranging from incidental ("Oops, I bought more pashmina than I needed for that cardigan") to slightly deranged ("That skein of Knit Collage Gypsy Garden was *literally* calling my name as I walked into the shop, so I had to buy it. In triplicate. In all ten colorways"). One species of stasher will inevitably look askance at the others, certain their reasons fall more into the category of "reasons" than others (insert eyeroll and scornful *pfffft* here). But is there more that binds us than separates us? Can math provide a counterpoint to answers that rely solely on illogical emotion? With the help of the online fiber-craft community Ravelry, I rustled up some numbers to see if they would lend any clarity to the matter.

However, before we take a soul-searching sift through the stats about stashes and us stashers, let's first give some consideration to the word itself. *Stash*, the noun, entered our American English vernacular in 1914, with decidedly criminal overtones. Someone who stashed a stash was likely a thief, squirreling away stolen goods. You could also stash your stash in a stash—that is, hole the loot up in your hideout. Although it took only a few decades for *stash* to be sanitized of intimations of illegal activity, contemporary yarn stashers, when discussing their . . . we'll call them *collections* . . . can often feel as though they are confessing some wrongdoing, without any clear understanding of the nature of their crime.

What is it we fear we might be guilty of? Let's have a look.

It's hard to know for sure what percentage of all knitters are also stashers. We do know that a mere 5 percent of Ravelry's 6.6 million users (some 307,000 knitters, weavers, and crocheters total) are stashers—or rather, use Ravelry to publicly track (or admit to) their stash. The numbers seem to further indicate that the greatest American stashers, by a long shot, are Californian—almost double the next demographics, of New Yorkers, or Texans. The largest group of non-English-speaking stashers are German, followed by French, then a succession of Scandinavians.

As temperatures and humidity rise, the number of stashers drops precipitously, but they're still in evidence: there are two stashers each in Guam, American Samoa, and the Federated States of Micronesia. There's one each in an impressively diverse assemblage of international locales, including Niger, Côte d'Ivoire, the Maldives, Saint Kitts and Nevis, Liechtenstein, Vatican City, Kosovo, Bouvet Island, East Timor, Botswana, French Southern and Antarctic Lands, Vanuatu, Tonga, Kyrgyzstan, Aruba, Saint Lucia, Northern Mariana Islands, Heard and McDonald Islands, Sri Lanka, Togo, Tuvalu, New Caledonia, the Falkland Islands, the Seychelles, South Georgia and the South Sandwich Islands, Tunisia, Niue, the Marshall Islands, Cuba, Madagascar, the British Virgin Islands, Haiti, and Albania. All by way of saying, pretty much anywhere in the world, if you run out of yarn and there is no local yarn store (LYS) available to you, chances are high that you'll find at least one human who can hook you up with a yarn fix.

Together, this very particular accumulation of Ravelry folk has more than 20,647,000 skeins of yarn logged into their virtual stashes. That averages out to more than sixty-eight skeins per person.

So far none of this sounds like the activity of nefarious masterminds, though.

Not if we assume that each one of these twenty million–plus skeins was come by legally (disappointingly, Ravelry doesn't track stolen skeins), either by purchase, gift or trade, or home-spinning. And not if we consider, too, that the aim of a stasher using the goods in his or her stash is to create hats—or mittens—or blankets—or socks, possibly with the further goal of giving them away as gifts. Yes, Ravelry stashers are sometimes looking to divest themselves of bits and pieces of their collections—some 53,000 of them are actively engaged in that pursuit as you read this. But on average, according to my in-house sources at Ravelry, they are probably more interested in using the site's stash function in order to figure out which skeins to yank out in preparation for the next work in progress (WIP). Why go through your whole collection manually when you can see it all tidy online, alongside already-completed projects, in various colorways, stitched up by your knitting compatriots?

All those stashed skeins weigh in at an incredible 8.4 million pounds—more than the combined heft of a small bridge, a drilling rig, a giant sequoia, and one blue whale. Unwind them and you've got almost 5 billion yards of yarn. Yeah, you read that right. Five billion yards. Which is 2.8 million miles. Ignoring weight and gauge, that's enough to knit 22 million socks. Or about four-and-a-half million medium-size women's sweaters.

Most of those socks (or sweaters) are probably going to be knit from yarn containing Merino or generic wool (more than 6.3 million stashed skeins) in the color blue (537,000 skeins) or green (443,000). Sock knitters will feel comfortable with the fact that the most popular stashed yarn weight is fingering or light fingering (3.2 million skeins).

All those stashed skeins weigh in at an incredible 8.4 million pounds—more than the combined heft of a small bridge, a drilling rig, a giant sequoia, and one blue whale. Unwind them and you've got almost 5 billion yards of yarn.

Sweater-fanciers will revel in this statistic: The combined total number of sport, DK, worsted, and Aran is a robust 5,070,148 skeins.

We appear to be less enthused about thread-weight hemp in yellow-green colorways—only one such skein is currently stashed—although we deem that slightly more desirable than the possibility of cobweb-weight qiviut or yak in shades of yellow-orange, currently not featured in any stash whatsoever.

Of the 10.2 million stash entries marked as "in stash" on Ravelry, there are an almost equal number that consist of one skein (3.9 million) and multiple skeins (3.8 million). Slightly more than 830,000 entries consist of less than an entire skein. What's the largest number of skeins anyone has tucked into their Ravelry stash? You will be either glad or very sorry you asked—regardless, the owner is doubtless someone you'd like to cozy up to. She or he is the proud stasher of 11,839 skeins of yarn; the next stasher in line has a still-impressive 11,522 skeins in his or her collection.

If these figures seem boggling or even worrisome, please consider the German word for stash: *vorrat*. Its translation is devoid of illicit overtones, rather connoting a stock or reserve of materials that a mindful person will need for some future purpose. As an added bonus, the

---

What's the largest number of skeins anyone has tucked into their Ravelry stash? You will be either glad or very sorry you asked— regardless, the owner is doubtless someone you'd like to cozy up to. She or he is the proud stasher of 11,839 skeins of yarn; the next stasher in line has a still-impressive 11,522 skeins in his or her collection.

term also happens to contain the word *rat*, which Austrian knitting designer Veronika Persché tells me literally means "advice." "So," she says, "it is a wise thing to build a vorrat, in order to be prepared in times of need."

Now, that's a definition to stash away and pull out if ever (whenever) our beloved co-dwellers demand to know exactly what the heck is going on here, and if it really requires the exclusive use of six closets, the guest bedroom, and the entire garage. "It's not illegal to stash yarn," you can assert with a straight face and a clear conscience. "And besides, I need this."

TRIPTYCH
BY STEPHANIE PEARL-MCPHEE

I

I am trying to do something about my stash because it has made its way into the kitchen again. I support, endorse, and love the idea of a stash that's whatever size your heart thinks it should be, but I also support and endorse the idea of being able to share your home with other humans if you so choose, and that you should be able to eat at the dining room table if that's your bag.

My stash is both large and mature. I am not a naturally tidy or organized person, so for the thing to stay usable, I need to admit that without some measure of organization (or the attempt at one, at the very least), the stash will begin oozing from room to room, becoming ever more chaotic and unstable. The system I have works pretty well—though as someone who constantly fights back against the part of her that owns two dead and dusty houseplants and is still knitting instead of doing something about that, it is inevitable that the stash will have some drift. New yarn often gets stuffed in a corner, a swatched and rejected yarn doesn't make it back into its correct spot, a mitten book (or seven) that I thumbed through while contemplating my choices ends up in the bathroom. Gradually, who I am and how infrequently I choose cleaning as an activity starts to exert itself, entropy takes over, and the stash springs free of its moorings.

I have accepted I am never going to live in the kind of home that you would see in a magazine, unless the magazine is running a contest that has something to do with the maximum amount of cat hair that can get stuck to a chair before a reasonable person does something about it. But I do try to keep the house just this side of a health code

I have accepted I am never going to live in the kind of home that you would see in a magazine, unless the magazine is running a contest that has something to do with the maximum amount of cat hair that can get stuck to a chair before a reasonable person does something about it.

violation. I'll be damned, though, if I can figure out how to keep the stash restrained enough that it's not the thing people gape at when they arrive and talk about when they leave.

I sometimes watch this TV show *Hoarders: Buried Alive*. I don't really enjoy it, but it triggers fear-based cleaning behavior in me, and that's valuable. In one episode, the hoarder was a knitter, and, while I admit that the rest of her house had a lot of problems, when the professional organizer assigned to make her home livable showed up, the first thing she went after was the stash. "Four pairs of size-six needles?" she shrieked, shocked and unbelieving. "Twenty balls of yarn! All blue!" She was appalled, and the woman was ashamed, and I had no idea what to do with any of my feelings because I am pretty sure I have more yarn than the knitter on that show. As a matter of fact, I am totally confident that I have a lot more than four pairs of size-six needles—and while I can agree that I shouldn't keep my blue yarn in the bathroom or next to a stack of empty pizza boxes that goes to the ceiling, I haven't ever considered it excessive.

I watched in horror as this organizer tried to convince the knitter that she needed less yarn and fewer needles. I felt a little unglued. I wanted to intervene, to tell them that she's being so misunderstood as an artist. I wanted to explain her choices, to say that she's going to go on to knit for a long time and that this stash is just good planning and choices, not hoarding. I wanted to ask her if this is what she would say if her client were a painter. Would she be allowed to keep just one canvas? Would they tell her it was silly to have fourteen sizes of brushes and ask her to choose the two she wanted to keep? Would they tell her that she simply couldn't have so many blue paints? That she'd have to decide between cerulean, navy, midnight, cobalt, and phthalo? Limit her ability to express herself for the sake of tidiness? My feelings got bigger and I got angrier, but part of me wondered: Do I want to defend this stash so that mine is defensible? Instead of cleaning up the stash and shoving it back into the spaces that it should be in, do I want to pretend that my knitting can't be or shouldn't be cleaned up, so that I don't have to admit that I'd rather be knitting than doing the work it would take to tidy it? Is this why I bought that poster that said, A CLEAN HOUSE IS A SIGN OF A WASTED LIFE?

This knitter on the show was hearing that she had too much yarn. Mostly, I think the larger issue was that she hadn't taken a bag of garbage to the bin in seventeen years. If I were the "organizational expert," I would have started there, let me tell you, but I get that when you're storing twenty-two kilos of used paper towels in your guest room, people are going to get very critical about all your stuff.

I've heard from people that I have too much yarn. Often, they tell me that I have more yarn than I could use in a lifetime. I don't even know if they can define that. I know that to the uninitiated it might seem like a simple equation: how much you knit versus how much you buy. But that's not how it works—and not just because nobody knows how long I'll live or how much I will knit. They don't even know what I'm going to use it for.

Most of my yarn is for knitting, but some of it has a more complicated destiny as support staff: It is there to make me want to knit. It's absolutely possible that I need the green Merino to inform how I'll use the blue alpaca, and that ball of gorgeous variegated yarn? You bet I've had it for ten years, and I completely admit that it's a yarn pet. I have no intention of ever knitting it, but it's earning the real estate it takes up with how it makes me feel about knitting. It is the textile artist's equivalent of a painting hung on the wall. It's there to be beautiful and to help me dream of possibility.

I sigh and look at the yarn and projects scattered around my house, and I think about how I love the way other people's homes look. I love the idea of living in a house that is well managed and tidy. I would love it if my stash didn't keep creeping out of its confines to wind up ornamenting the kitchen, but I can't figure out how that's going to happen, as long as given any choice between tidying the stash and knitting with it, the latter is going to win most of the time. I think about cleaning it up, but don't you think I would be spending all my time organizing the stash instead of working with it—and that this would make it ridiculous to own?

My stash isn't just the stuff I'm going to knit. It's how I think about knitting and, frankly, some inspiration takes up more room than you'd imagine.

II

I am trying to do something about my stash. I've just finished culling it, an event that is practically a religious holiday in this house. Culling the stash is something I started doing about ten years ago, when I had to admit that more yarn was coming into the house than was going out, and that the math on that was pretty hard to ignore. If you buy twenty skeins of sock yarn a year, and you knit only ten pairs of socks per year, you're going to have a very compelling problem in a short period of time. I have absolutely no problem defending my yarn buying. Knitting is what I love, and it is normal, human, and smart to surround yourself with the things that make you happy and give you choices and inspiration. It is not normal to bury yourself over the course of twenty years without fighting back a little bit, even as you can see it happening. Now during the cull, I actually get rid of yarn.

Most of my yarn is for knitting, but some of it has a more complicated destiny as support staff: It is there to make me want to knit.

Some of it goes to charity, some of it gets re-homed to friends and family who will actually use it, but during the cull, the stash flow at my house reverses itself, and yarn, books, and needles leave the house.

I don't do it just because of space, because I can't end up sleeping in the bathtub, or because I can't manage my feelings about knitting and the yarn it results in. I do it because yarn sometimes finds its way into this house without deliberate and careful thought, and without curation, without a chance to reverse the recklessness that sometimes brings yarn here, the stash starts to weigh on me. It lurks around the house, looming darkly and making me feel bad.

I'm not sure what the bad feeling is, but I used to wonder if it was guilt. It would make sense; the stash is obviously an excess, and when it's at its largest there are definitely things in it that won't get used. It's more than I need, and squeezing another skein into a shelf that's already packed feels a little like scraping half a pie into the compost while children are starving in Africa. I don't feel bad about having what I need, but I sure feel a little uncomfortable about having more than I can use and letting the potential in the yarn go to waste as it gathers dust.

I thought maybe the feeling was of responsibility, some sort of culpability for having been the person who brought all this here, in whatever deranged moment of weakness unhinged me. Even if I can see now that I got that purple mohair only because it was 50 percent off, am I required to execute the penance of knitting it? If a tower of sock yarn is getting big enough to topple in the night and bury me so deeply that it will be three days before they can excavate my lifeless form, do I have to keep trying to use it up, just to avoid admitting I bought that last skein to compliment the dyer? If I made this bed, is it necessary that I have to knit it?

Then there's what I do for a living. I'm a member of the knitting industry, and sometimes people give me their yarn, or they're happy to see me buy it. I like pleasing them, and I know they hope I might knit it and they will have a little lovely publicity. I know this, and I want to help them, but I'm one person, and I worry that somewhere, they're sitting in their living room, reading my blog, and thinking, "Dammit, when is she going to knit my yarn?," and I'm sitting in my stash room, looking at the same skein, only it's next to 470 others, and I feel like I'm obligated to knit all of them really, really soon, and the next thing I know I'm feeling really sweaty.

It could be one of those reasons; it might be something else. Perhaps it's possible for all that potential just to get to be too much for me. There is a mystical moment when I have more yarn than psychic energy, and it doesn't feel good anymore. It feels like a burden, and it feels like the stash isn't something I've chosen. When that happens, it's time for a cull. I have to go into the stash, look at the yarn that's come into my life, and ask myself if it still has a right to be here. If it can't be defended in my court, where the judge is kind and generous but firm, then it's time for the yarn in question to make its way into someone else's stash.

I get a few boxes out—one for my knitting friends, one to donate—and I start going through the stash. The thing that amazes me while I'm at it is that every single skein I pick up and hold, every item—whether it was a gift or an impulse buy or a moment of weakness in the face of a ridiculous discount—all of this, no matter how it came to be here, at the time that it came into the stash, when I first held it in my hands, I wholly believed it was going to be the next thing I knit.

As I work, I try to let go of the feelings of obligation, responsibility, and commitment and look honestly at twelve balls of bulky mint-green brushed Merino that I bought in 1985 and quietly admit that my tastes have changed. I don't want that batwing sweater anymore, even if it means I wasted the money. I go through it all, sorting and deciding, and I keep going until the stash feels like what it's supposed to be, which is a pleasure. Anything that's not going to be knit by me or loved by me, or that can't explain to me exactly why it's here . . . that stuff moves on so that someone can enjoy it, and I can stop resenting it for being the physical embodiment of my inability to grow as a person.

I admit that my stash is large, I admit that there are a lot of reasons for yarn to be in it, and I admit that I am weak in the face of yarn. I admit it all, and I cull ruthlessly so my stash reflects who I am, because otherwise, my stash makes me feel bad.

III

I am trying to do something about my stash, to bring it in line with my personal manifesto, but I'll be the first to admit that it's not going very well. I say that I let yarn go, that I release things, that I have a vision of what my stash should be. I really believe that a stash should be a source of inspiration, motivation, and the root of creativity for a textile artist. I believe in keeping things that aren't going to be knit now, or even maybe ever, as long as they are part of your personal vision. Every skein or ball should be chosen and deliberate. I don't even think a stash can be technically too big, as long as it fits within the rules, you haven't had a visit from the local authorities who want to talk about reining it in enough so that firefighters can get to you in an emergency, and the practice hasn't negatively affected your credit rating.

Here I stand then, trying to take charge of this whole thing and keep it within the confines of my system. I am holding a ball of yarn that breaks every rule that I have and, according to all the criteria I have ever set, should be in the box I'm giving away, but I can't do it. I cannot let it go. It's one of a whole bunch of skeins that make no sense if you know me—odd yarns that you wouldn't expect to find here, that I would never buy, that don't reflect who I am as an artist, that don't contribute to my work, won't be knit, aren't inspiring, and, technically, don't reflect the way that I like to interact with my stash.

They're wild cards, with no right to be here. For example, the yarn I'm holding is variegated, with all the colors of the rainbow in it. It is dominated by a shiny filament of fake silver and a bright pink color—saccharine sweet, girly, and intense. That pink is the color of lipstick nobody buys, and not only would I never wear it, I dislike the color enough that I wouldn't even knit it for a friend who was misguided enough to think she liked it. That should be enough to get it out of here, never mind that it is a fantastically crappy acrylic. It is a yarn that you would never, ever associate with me. It's a yarn that might belong to a child who tells you that her favorite color is sparkle rainbow.

One warm day in June, about twenty years ago, when my daughters were very little, they brought me a birthday present. It was wrapped in tinfoil (very smart—you don't need tape that way) and a bit sticky. They presented it to me with pride, their little faces glowing with the delight of what they saw as a very well-executed plan. I pried open the packet, and inside was that ball of yarn, glittering brilliantly in the sunshine. They'd taken their own money, gone to the store, thought long and hard about what to get me, and settled on this particular gem. Now, true empathy is a late-blooming flower, so they didn't quite get the details right, but I still remember the way that they showed me how pink it was, how shiny it was, and explained, essentially, how it was a moonbeam of beauty, the apex of elegance. I stood there, holding a ball of yarn that was exactly what you'd get if Barbie and My Little Pony dropped acid and tried to come up with a colorway, and even though it was the exact opposite of everything I like in a yarn, I loved it. It was the first time my children tried to give me a gift that reflected who I am. I can no sooner get rid of that yarn than I can set fire to their baby pictures.

There is a mystical moment when I have more yarn than psychic energy, and it doesn't feel good anymore. It feels like a burden, and it feels like the stash isn't something I've chosen. When that happens, it's time for a cull.

In another box are twenty-four balls of absolutely terrible yarn that my husband bought for me in China. In an afternoon that ended up a lot more complicated and expensive than he ever intended it to be, he took the time to find out where in the vast market you buy yarn, and he went there—way out of his way, navigating a country and a language he didn't know, to try to please me. It's true that when he found the yarn he panicked and opted for quantity over quality, but how do you send a gesture of love like that to charity? Horrific pantyhose shade of taupe or not, I am emotionally stuck to that big lot of yarn.

Those three over there, the ones that are neon colors, are a gift from a family friend. On her last trip here from Japan, she unloaded a great big basket of gifts from her home. Everyone got tea and rice candies and green tea–flavored everything, but I got Japanese yarn. That small white ball is all that's left of the yarn I used for my eldest daughter's baby blanket. The oatmeal-colored skeins that are about as soft as twine? I bought them at a tiny yarn shop in the basement of a house in Newfoundland, on one of the first trips my husband and I ever took together. The small ball of acid-green polyester is all that remains of the stash of my paternal grandmother—the woman who taught me how to knit. The eight balls of tweedy red yarn with odd electric-blue flecks that shreds when you try to knit it? Those are the legacy of a friend who had to give up knitting and passed them into my safekeeping, sure that I could somehow fulfill their destiny. Each monstrosity is a postcard, a treasure, and makes up a scrapbook of an unusually bulky sort.

I know what my stash is supposed to be, and mostly, it's that. My stash is useful, it is inspiration, it is the groundwork for my art, it is the magic box of paints and tools into which I reach to make things. It is my own personal store, a curated collection of things that make my knitting life possible and let me start mittens at 1:00 AM, should the magic strike me. It's the insurance policy that will let me keep knitting even if I run out of money, sheep stop bearing wool, or a zombie apocalypse closes every yarn shop in the world . . . but my stash is not just that.

It is also memento, remembrance, and souvenir. An expression of not just what I want to make but also who I am, who I love, where I've been, and who loves me. I'll keep as much of it as I want to, even if it's rainbow sparkle.

WITHOUT A STASH
BY AMY HERZOG

Hello! My name is Amy. I am an avid knitter, and I have no stash.

The casual observer in my home might argue with that statement. It's true, there's certainly some yarn here. But the yarn in my house is not a stash.

Any knitter can tell you that "having a stash" isn't simply another way of saying you "own some yarn." There are as many reasons to stash as there are stashers, but every stasher *does* have a reason. They've chosen each hank of yarn in their stash for a particular purpose, and stashes are uniquely personal as a result.

Knitters' stashes are both a story they tell themselves about their knitting and the means with which to live out that story.

The yarn in my house is different. It fills a generous handful of little cube bins in my studio. It's a hodgepodge: remnants from past projects, sample hanks for future projects, and my next six to nine months of design work. All of that yarn is lovely. Much of it is carefully chosen. But none of it is my stash.

I know this because I was once as avid a stasher as I am a knitter.

I picked up knitting for the second time as a young adult after several obnoxious teenage years in which I felt I was "too cool" for the fiber arts. My reacquaintance with knitting was uniquely tied to that time in my life: I wanted to connect to a core part of my mother's life after she passed away when I was twenty-one. Knitting helped me sit quietly next to my new spouse as we watched a movie or TV in the evenings; it also channeled my intense desire to make things and be creative, which wasn't getting much of an outlet in my day job.

I became a stasher almost immediately. My stash was a crisp and focused plan, reflected in the name of my first knitting blog: *stash, knit, repeat.* The story my small, tidy stash told (along with its spreadsheet) was a step-by-careful-step crafting plan. I knit through the stash and replenished it regularly. Obsessing over, fondling, and working through that teeny stash gave me so much joy.

After a few years, my life changed and my relationship with my stash did, too. I had my first child and moved across the country to follow a professorship for my husband, which gave me the chance to stop working for a time. I packed up that tidy little stash into a single box and moved it with me. The story my stash started to tell was a calming one, the familiar hanks soothing me through the changes and uncertainty of that time.

Then, when I lost five family members over a brutal eight months, my stash's story changed again: It became an ongoing attempt to find beauty still left in the world, a solemn promise to be part of that beauty even when I was feeling most bereft. This change in my stash's story started slowly. When my aunt passed unexpectedly, I found a new hand-dyed lace-weight, drank in its saturated color, smelled the crisp tang of the silk, and then transformed it into a complex shawl that became more than the sum of its parts.

Then when Lois, the grandmother who was also my crafting mentor, died, I made a furious and intense commitment to knit as much as I possibly could, as quickly as I possibly could. This rich, intense hank would be lacy socks I could wear on cold winter mornings. That plump, smooth wool would transform into an adorable toddler sweater for a dear friend's little one. I'd make hanks of ultrasoft cotton into warm caps for my remaining grandmother to wear in the fall. I tried, through my stash, to capture both my own creative urge and Lois's.

When both of my grandfathers followed my aunt and my grandmother, the story of my stash got more frantic, as I tried to reconnect to the past I was losing. I scrambled to find the earthy goodness of a rustic wool. Smelling it transported me back to a cold snowy afternoon, with tiny crusty icicles melting into a comfortable smell by my grandfather's woodstove. I don't remember how old I was, but the raised stone hearth was the perfect size to sit on, basking in the warmth of the air and the stones. I was consumed by the search for the perfect colors to re-create an old stranded sweater, keeping me warm as I scrambled over granite ledges and crunched leaves while trailing after my other grandfather, walking around his land.

By the time I lost a baby in my second trimester, life felt out of control. The purchase of a soft, fine wool was a dual-edged sword, reminding me of other tiny beings in my family who hadn't survived . . . and yet also declaring my hope that another child would be born. I buried my losses in my first trip to Rhinebeck, barely noticing anything as I shoveled hank after hank into my bag.

My stash exploded during those eight months, quickly filling bin after bin, shelf after shelf.

I desperately needed the stories I told myself with that stash. I desperately needed the healing it gave me, and I don't judge myself harshly for that tumultuous time. But as the brutality faded and life settled down, I started to notice the rather large amount of yarn that now surrounded me. It became clear that in my heart of hearts, this giant stash wasn't telling the right story for me.

Once it lost the deep emotional connection to the grieving process, much of the yarn I'd purchased just didn't look as enticing as it had. The story of that grief-stricken stash changed. I was left with a story of suffocating obligation, and past pain, and old responsibilities.

The financial needs of having two preschoolers gave me the push I needed to address the mental weight of that accumulated yarn: My yarn budget became a shadow of its former self, and I started knitting through my stash. I made some purchases, of course—at a festival or from a dyer introduced to me by a friend. I knit things up quickly, and my stash kept shrinking.

Eventually, there was hardly anything left.

It felt so amazing.

In a life otherwise filled with appointments and routines and responsibilities, my diminishing and eventually nonexistent stash gave me mental permission to break out of plans and constraints and indulge in whimsy instead—to change my mind a billion times with no consequence except the joy of being able to change my mind a billion times.

Without a stash, my yarn purchasing became immediate, the hanks transforming into pieces reflecting who I was at that particular instant. I quickly worked a smooth wool-silk blend into a sleek spring cardigan to match that great skirt I'd just purchased. One fall, we discovered a new hiking trail; I found a nubby, rustic woolen-spun and whipped it up into a cabled pullover I could wear on the trail with my family. The next summer, I was headed to the ocean for a weekend, but nights are cold up in Maine, so I dashed to the store for my favorite hemp blend and pulled together a beachy sweatshirt.

When I was in a place where my knitting urges focused on others, my stashless projects told that story, too. My eldest came home from kindergarten one day begging for knee socks. We hit the local fiber festival to find sock yarn that screamed "Jacob," and he proudly slipped them on the second they were off my needles. I have a fantastic picture of his giant, silly grin as he posed on one leg for the camera. My always-chilly husband shaves his head, and a quick drop in temperatures one cold November Saturday sent me running for a hank of his favorite cashmere blend. I'd finished a little indoor cap by the end of the night, much to his delight.

And on, and on, and on.

In my years without a stash, I've discovered something beautiful. When I got rid of the yarn that bound me to previous versions of myself, my *projects* were finally able to tell the story I spent years trying (and failing) to articulate with my stash.

It turns out that the most important parts of my fiber life were never about the stash. The bits of my family, myself, and my friends that I tried to work into yarn purchases got tangled up in history and baggage and stale expectations instead. Their stories fell flat. These bits of me and my loved ones couldn't be blended into hanks of yarn on a shelf. They needed to be blended into my creations instead.

The story those creations tell is so much more satisfying than anything my stash ever said to me. Now everything I create is rooted entirely in where I am at that particular time—some items reflect on what has come before, some zing crazily to the side, some are lavish and some sturdily simple. The things I've made since I stopped stashing make an authentic, beautiful story of the women I've been, the people I've loved, and the life I've led.

I know what a stash can do for a person. I deeply, respectfully understand it. But I'm vastly happier without one.

The careful reader will probably remember that I admitted to having a decently large chunk of yarn in my house. And it's fair to ask: If that yarn isn't a stash, what on earth is it?

The truth is, it's just yarn. My knitting story got a bit more complicated about five years ago, when I started designing professionally. The yarn in my house got a bit more complicated, too.

At first, the switch to designing resulted in a huge influx of yarn. My first book had twenty-one adult-size sweaters in it, and let me tell you: The week all that yarn showed up was a pretty daunting one. My work for magazines—more yarn. My own pattern line—more yarn.

Things really got out of hand when I realized that I had even more control over the yarn-design marriage than I'd originally thought. *Wait a minute: I can speak directly with a yarn company about what a particular idea wants, and then the exact yarn I need for this exact idea shows up at my house, made just for me?! The perfect result of a creative collaboration? YES PLEASE!*

The yarn was back. Briefly.

That heady influx of yarn slowed down and got used up pretty quickly. Yarns tend to turn over rapidly, with something getting discontinued pretty much every season. And nobody wants a new pattern to call for a yarn that's already been discontinued. I was soon back to acquiring yarn and knitting it up almost immediately.

I do tend to keep more yarn around the house than I did before I started designing, because at this point in my career, I plan my design schedule out about a year. In the interest of helping you understand why I still consider myself a stashless knitter, here's a brief tour of what's in those bins:

- The smallest amount of yarn is detritus from past projects. I try to acquire generous enough yardage that I have a lot of design flexibility; that almost always results in a hank or three left over at the end of a project. Those leftovers collect until they outgrow their bin, at which point I donate/review/hold a contest/give the yarn to someone who can do something lovely with it.
- Next in terms of actual quantity is swatching yarn: sample hanks, both full-size and mini, for swatching and planning out the next set of projects and collaborations.
- Finally, there are the sweater quantities. They represent a small(ish) number of projects, a giant amount of yardage, and somewhere between six and twelve months of work. This yarn—between eight and twenty sweaters' worth—comes from businesses I believe in and represents the best our industry has to offer. Much of it is chosen strategically to make a coherent and easily acquired portfolio of garments. A very few sweaters' worth is yarn that caused me to squeal with delight and grab it with greedy hands the second I saw it. (I try to keep creative juices flowing by giving myself an immediate "just because" project every season.)

All told, the yarn in my house probably totals one to two giant plastic bins. It will all be gone within a year. Most of it says very little that's uniquely personal to me. It's stunningly beautiful; but if it all disappeared tomorrow, I'd just shrug and make a new work plan. It's lovely yarn, and I enjoy working with it, but at the end of the day, it's an (especially) inspiring set of work materials. It's not a stash. And I wouldn't have it any other way.

In the nearly twenty years since I picked my knitting needles back up again, in this one tiny little part of my life, I've lost myself in the pure joy of ephemera. I get great pleasure out of the freedom to make my crafty tomorrow whatever I'd like it to be when I get there.

Maybe I'll want to dive into a series of lace wraps, or more knee socks for the boys (who are rapidly becoming young men), or a lap blanket, or a cozy hat, or a sweater like the ones my mother made us when we were kids, or something inspired by that top I've finally worn to death . . .

. . . or maybe not. Maybe I'll want to do something I can't even conceive of now.

I'll figure it out when I get there. I don't need to plan for it. I don't want to plan for it. I don't want to shackle tomorrow's creativity to the place I'm in today. There will be yarn that's perfect for whatever is captivating me at the moment. Or not, and I'll move on to something else. It's all good.

My name is Amy. I'm an avid knitter with no stash—and no desire to acquire one. Who would have thought?

THE LIFE-CHANGING MAGIC OF KEEPING IT ALL
BY ANN SHAYNE

I'm tidying. I'm doing the thing with the stuff that Marie Kondo is telling me to do. Listening to the audiobook of *The Life-Changing Magic of Tidying Up* is, frankly, like enduring a sweet-voiced nag session from the cubicle mate you never really liked. I know. I know I know *I know*.

Marie Kondo is, however, onto something.

Her instructions: Hold each item in my hands. Does it spark joy? Keep. No joy sparked? Discard. Repeat until I have laid hands on every single item in my house. Put the items I love back into my home in an orderly way. Because of this tidying, my life will now be forever changed. I will end up either divorced, more deeply in love with my husband, or going to nursing school.

But Marie Kondo doesn't ever discuss that category that we knitters hold in a super-special, 99-percent-irrational, and deeply felt place: the yarn.

I am here to humbly explain the life-changing magic of tidying your stash. There are two strategies. They are polar opposites, so it is guaranteed that one of these will work for you, or you can toggle back and forth between the two methods. Your life will now be forever changed. Get ready for nursing school; this is big stuff.

But Marie Kondo doesn't ever discuss that category that we knitters hold in a super-special, 99-percent-irrational, and deeply felt place: the yarn.

Method 1: Shock and Awe. Scrape up every ball, skein, hank, and cone of yarn, and dump it all in a forty-gallon Hefty trash bag—or two, I don't judge. Hold the bag in your hands. Do not wonder for a moment whether there is joy to be found in that bag. Just drag it out of your life with a big sayonara. The goal: Keep absolutely no stash at all. When you have the impulse to knit, go buy some yarn. It will be brand new, thrilling, and exactly the thing you have in mind for the project you want to make. You will never waste time on ill-conceived knitting projects involving eight kinds of cream-colored yarn bought over the course of fifteen years.

Method 2: Bring It On. The Bring It On Method rejects the fundamental exercise of asking yourself whether your yarn sparks joy. OF COURSE IT SPARKS JOY: IT'S YARN, AND I LOVE TO KNIT. Keep tremendous piles of yarn in furniture not designed for yarn storage. Put yarn in parts of the house you rarely visit, so that you are sometimes surprised by purchases you made in 2009 somewhere in Arkansas. Make sure that much of this yarn is purchased on vacations, so that it is all larded up with sentiment and emotion and meaning, to the point where you weep slightly when recalling the now defunct yarn shop where you bought it. Also be certain to include hard-won batches of yarn, like from fierce eBay auctions, or the two skeins of Shade 209 Minestrone you begged off a kindly Ravelry member so that you could complete your exhausting Fair Isle project (which you still haven't completed).

If you feel like spending quality time with your yarn without having to make anything, I'll leave you with some questions to answer as you gaze upon the bounty of your stash. The Bring It On Method does have opinions about certain yarn situations, but feel free to ignore them. You may be moved to discard some of your yarn, but if not, who cares? You've got all this fantastic yarn!

Does it have a handwritten tag? Keep. How could you even think of not having that yarn?

Does it live inside a Liberty of London bag? Keep. It means you got to London. Wallow in that forever.

Do you have multiple batches of yarn in the same color? Keep. Isn't it cool how subtly different they are? Only a connoisseur like you can see the immense differences between two brands of four-ply yarn in green. Is that a bit of chartreuse in there? Sigh.

Is it sock weight? Keep. Just keep it.

Is it mauve? I know, right? Who invented mauve yarn? Get rid of it!

And finally . . .

Is it lace-weight? Keep. I call this knitting-through-the-apocalypse yarn. Prepper yarn. When the end times come, fine-weight knitting is going to be the thing, because all the yarn stores will be obliterated, Wi-Fi will be the stuff of myth and memory, and you're going to need fine-gauge, analog knitting for the long haul. Remember: There will be no sheep. Plan accordingly.

FULL CIRCLE WITH THE TRAVELING STASH
BY GUDRUN JOHNSTON

As I sit down to write about my stash, I realize that doing so means more than writing about the cedar chest I've stuffed to bursting with yarn. Really, my concept of *stash* extends beyond that—beyond the skeins of yarn themselves. It encompasses the variety of treasured knitting-related things that I carry with me. Some of these things are actual objects, even family heirlooms. Some are less physically tangible. My stash includes family history. It's about memories of my childhood and of my children's childhood. It's about the crazy journey life has been for me and my husband, and it's about the items I've carried with me along the way. In order to write about my stash, I need to give you a little background.

First, I should explain that I like to move. Or is it that I *need* to move? Maybe both, but in any event I've moved a lot over the years. This has affected everything I'm likely to talk about here. I'm restless, always caught between longing for my original home in Scotland and for the wild and wonderful places on offer when I married my husband, an American. For better or worse, my husband shares my wanderlust. That's why he happened to be in Edinburgh to meet me in the first place. As a young couple, we managed to travel largely with what we could carry. We'd fill a few duffel bags with clothes, and we'd cram a bunch of books and whatnot into surface mail bags and send them out to sea, to catch up with us a month or so down the line. Thus we hopped from Edinburgh to Annapolis, bought a tiny Toyota truck with a cab that we could sleep in, and drove all the way across America to the West Coast, where we hopscotched from place to place. Eugene. Portland. Sunny California! Good times.

It was a wonderfully freeing time. We were able to uproot and fly on a whim, to chase whatever dream or passion captured us at the time. But this went both ways. It wasn't long before we got hungry for old stuff like castles and cobblestone streets and prawn cocktail crisps and warm ale. We headed back to Europe, first to a loft apartment in Albertville, France, and then home to rural Scotland, where the family started to grow. Before long we had two children, spaced eighteen months apart.

Did they make it harder to travel? Did they anchor us? Nope. Our kids were born with feet on both continents. They both had two passports before they had any say in the matter, and they put them to use pretty much straightaway. We'd bundle them up, with the toys and the car seats and hap shawl blankets, and be off again. It's almost embarrassing how many times we've relocated across the Atlantic, and across the breadth of America. Thank god for audio books for those long car journeys! My daughter, Maya, was born in rural Perthshire, Scotland, but she learned to crawl in South Lake Tahoe and took her first steps in Western Massachusetts. My son, Sage, came into the world in a little yellow house in New England, began crawling in Basalt, Colorado, and got up on his pegs in Dunkeld, Scotland.

All that youthful traveling was great fun in many ways. It also had a hand in changing the course of my professional and creative life. When Maya was born, my mother, Patricia Johnston, commissioned a traditional Shetland hap for her. It was beautiful—a delicate cream-colored yarn worked in a fine lace pattern. It was, perhaps, a bit *too* delicate. It didn't last nearly long enough. I, having only knit a bit as a girl and not for years since, didn't catch the signs that it was about to unravel spectacularly. So that was that.

Fortunately, a kind relative had yet another shawl made. This one was a sturdier variety. No lace at all. Colorful instead of subtle. Maya loved it. She slept with it. Walked with it. Lived with it. She had it in hand almost constantly. It was a faithful companion—perhaps more treasured than any of her numerous teddies and various dolls—through the first years of her life.

That, of course, means that it also traveled with us. That blanket navigated airports and train stations and buses and roadside pit stops just as we did. There were more than a few near-misses with losing it. The shawl stuffed in a corner of a seat in a diner. Nearly left behind when we rushed off to a shuttle, hauling our luggage to the airport. Briefly abandoned at the gate when our delayed flight finally began boarding. Left in the wrong terminal during a stopover on some blurry-eyed overnight flight. Eventually, crossing the Atlantic once again via the northern route that stopped over in Iceland, the shawl succeeded in slipping away from us. I'd like to think that some fashionably dressed Icelandic girl or boy adopted it. Let's assume so, and let's assume it gave them some of the joy and comfort that it had given Maya.

For my part, I had a distraught daughter on my hands, suffering through what was perhaps the first significant loss of her life. She was inconsolable. The blanket had to be replaced, but not just any replacement would do. It had to be special. I decided that this time I'd knit something for her myself. As I mentioned, my only previous knitting experience had been as a girl. That, obviously, was years prior. Still, I found a pattern for a simple poncho, which Maya liked the look of. I picked up needles and yarn, and I hesitantly cast on and began. Maya watched as the poncho slowly took shape. I think watching the process helped her get invested in it, and watching her helped me to love the act of creating for her.

The finished result was no masterpiece, but it didn't need to be. It was a poncho, made by my hands for my daughter. She loved it. Again she had a knitted companion. This one she didn't lose, in part because she could throw it over her head and wear it, which had been part of the idea in the first place. As I write this Maya is seventeen years old, a young woman who is massively creative in her own right, a hard-working student on the verge of heading off to college. And she still has that poncho, now another well-traveled piece of knitwear that mostly sits on her pillow like a well-loved teddy bear.

And me? I'd rediscovered knitting. Little did I know how much that project was going to change and shape my life and career.

As the years passed it became harder and harder to travel light. We accumulated stuff. Things we couldn't pack into those duffels anymore. Things we didn't want to part with. My husband went from being a starving writer to being a published novelist, and he collected a lot of beloved books in the process. A literary stash. I went from being a novice knitter to being a full-time designer in a transformation that surprised me then and still does now. Along with this, of course, came yarn. Yarn and more yarn. My stash was born.

Considering that we're almost twenty years into marriage, with two teenage kids and a large dog (a Rhodesian Ridgeback), you'd think my family was a bit past this moving business, right? Well . . . not quite. Most recently we moved across the Atlantic, from Massachusetts to Edinburgh. And then we moved back to Massachusetts. Two moves in twelve months. Madness, I know.

We took everything with us in both directions. Well, *almost* everything. We left a baby grand piano in its place of origin on the last leg, but everything else we jammed into a shipping container. We filled it to the brim, closed the doors, and wished all the possessions of our lives bon voyage. Twice.

I think it's fair to say that we're expert packers at this point. Despite culling our bookshelves before departure, we still appeared to have an awful lot of books. However, putting just books in a box makes for heavy lifting and wastes precious nook and cranny space. We (I) also had an awful lot of yarn to pack, and I didn't really fancy having light, easily squashed boxes either. We took to mixing the boxes: books and yarn together, hard and soft, heavy and light. We've discovered the two have quite the happy marriage in a box. By the time we were done

I'll admit straight off that I am not one of those knitters who has rooms packed to overflowing with bins of yarn. I might've been, but, as you've been reading, I haven't sat still long enough to make that possible.

we had close to one hundred boxes with YARN and BOOKS scrawled in Sharpie across them. I guess that about sums us up.

I'll admit straight off that I am not one of those knitters who has rooms packed to overflowing with bins of yarn. I might've been, but, as you've been reading, I haven't sat still long enough to make that possible. Generally speaking, I don't purchase sweaters' quantities of yarn. I do the best I can to limit my stash. I'm not saying it's shabby; it's certainly not. But I try to restrict it to that cedar chest I mentioned earlier. I might've actually been able to stick to that, except . . . well, there's so much lovely yarn out there. It's a constant test of my resolve, never more so than on the Grand Shetland Adventure trips I run with Mary Jane Mucklestone. Among the many things we do is to stop in at the local yarn suppliers, like Jamieson's and J&S Woolbrokers. How could I possibly leave there empty-handed? So, in addition to my cedar chest, several plastic totes now attempt to contain the ever-growing overflow of Shetland yarn.

It's not just yarn that makes up my stash, though. I consider my inherited collection of vintage Shetland knitwear a significant part of that stockpile. Indeed, it's the most treasured part, made up of pieces that my mother designed and had knitted up locally in Shetland when she ran the original Shetland Trader back in the seventies. My siblings and I wore them as youngsters in Shetland. I've got the old photos to prove it! For me, these pieces mean so much on so many levels. They're reminders of my mother's creativity, of her style and verve and personality. They're composed not just of fiber but of memories from my earliest days in Shetland, a close-knit family often huddled in small cottages on remote isles in Shetland, on mainland Scotland, and on the tiny island of Rum in the Inner Hebrides. My parents couldn't stay in one place, either. It's really quite stunning to think of the thousands of miles these pieces have traveled, the vistas they've seen, the accents to which they've had to adjust.

Despite the wear we put them through as active kids, the garments were always carefully stored and passed down. They eventually came to me. Even before I'd started knitting, I loved the garments for the connection to my mother and to my childhood. About thirty years on, I got to watch my children bring my mother's designs to life again in a new incarnation. With my own designing and the rebirth of the Shetland Trader, these pieces tie together many of the most cherished components of my life.

One of the best things about my Shetland Trader vintage knitwear stash is that it continues to grow. Each trip back to Shetland unveils another piece of my mother's, lovingly preserved by some kind soul. Two unique sweaters combining Fair Isle and lace (and very seventies in appearance—think bell sleeves and dramatic turtlenecks) showed up at the home of Wendy Inkster in Shetland. She'd acquired them at a local sale, immediately recognized the Shetland Trader label, and thankfully chose to keep them as display pieces in her studio. Wendy makes adorable bears from recycled Fair Isle sweaters. Thank goodness in this case she chose to keep these sweaters as display pieces! Even more, she generously passed them on to me. Friends of my mother

It's not just yarn that makes up my stash, though. I consider my inherited collection of vintage Shetland knitwear a significant part of that stockpile.

have also told me of the pieces they still own of hers. Most recently, I found out about a full-length dress she'd designed, one I've never seen in person. It's been wonderful to find other people acknowledging the artistry and cultural import of my mother's work, protecting it with as much care as I do.

Moving forward also brought me full circle, with my stash speaking to the future as well as attesting to the past. My next pattern collection will focus on my mother's work. While the garments have been handed down to me, the patterns for them weren't. So my intention is to create patterns to bring the vintage designs back to life for today's knitters. I may throw in some alterations and touches of my own, but I'm really attracted to the notion of making these pieces living garments that are being knitted into being yet again, the soft clicking of needles attesting to their rebirth.

And that, really, is what my stash is all about. It's the inspiration that pushes me to want to share Shetland's knitting tradition with as much of the world as I can. It's a deeply personal calling, one that I was born into and gifted by my parents. Actually, there's even a bit of prescience in the name. *The Shetland Trader* was originally the name of a ship. Right from the start our mission has been crossing waters to make connections. As that's the case, it's clear my traveling days aren't over yet.

THE MINIMALIST SPEAKS
BY KAY GARDINER

Several times a year, someone of my acquaintance asks me to teach her to knit. I say "sure," all casual-like and butter-wouldn't-melt. I take care not to spook a nascent knitter by jumping up and down and chanting, "New knitter! New knitter! New knitter!"

We make a date for the knitter-in-training to come to my apartment, and the new knitter then says, "Tell me what to buy and bring over to your place, so that I can learn." And I start laughing like a loon.

I could teach thirty people to knit on ten minutes' notice with materials close to hand. And I'm a minimalist. My stash is no stash at all compared to many of the Stashes I've Seen. But I am well provisioned for any occasion requiring knitting.

Poor, sweet, innocent baby knitters. They imagine that they will knit something, and that when they have finished that thing, they will then do a bit of research to determine what they might knit next. Then, and only then, will they go out and buy materials to knit one more thing. That is not how knitting works, for me or for any other knitter I know. When it comes to yarn, supply quickly overtakes demand.

New knitters do not have a clue. If this knitting thing takes hold, their home, like mine, will inexorably fill up with the tools and materials of knitting: needles in every size and length of cable, stitch markers under sofa cushions, scissors in every drawer, and, most of all, yarn. Yarn to the rafters. Yarn in my closet. Yarn in everyone else's closets. Yarn in the enamel-over-steel covered roasting pan that only gets used at Thanksgiving and Christmas. Shopping bags of yarn that I have to step over every night to draw the blinds in my bedroom.

Matisse had a lot of canvases. Many tubes of paint. That little Cézanne he couldn't afford but bought anyway. A dead butterfly that was the right shade of cobalt blue. His place was a mess. If you're really into something, there's no shame in having supplies.

Matisse had a lot of canvases. Many tubes of paint. That little Cézanne he couldn't afford but bought anyway. A dead butterfly that was the right shade of cobalt blue. His place was a mess. If you're really into something, there's no shame in having supplies.

A person on the cusp of becoming a knitter doesn't know how appealing yarn is. How a skein of good wool can speak to you, how it can embody a memory or beckon from the future, how—like a brilliant blue butterfly—it can fill you with enthusiasm even if you never take off the ballband.

Given all this, how on earth can I think of myself as a minimalist?

I grew up in a tidy, aluminum-sided house with no tchotchkes, no bookshelves. No extra chairs. No posters on the wall of the bedroom I shared with my sister, in which a pair of novice nuns would have felt quite at home. Cleanliness and order were the guiding principles of our tribe, which descended from various Northern European and Scandinavian people who lived simply in small spaces because they had no choice in the matter. To me, bare floorboards provide their own kind of comfort, especially if they are redolent of Johnson Paste Wax. Although my life today is filled with books and yarn, I feel uneasy when the objects overflow.

Periodically, at least once a year, I want to burn it all down. I go around to all my hidey-holes and remove the yarn. I empty bags and bins of wool onto my bed. I go through it all, one crammed Ziploc bag at a time, asking myself whether I still love this yarn, do I have any earthly idea of what I will make with it, whether it's cheering me up or laying me low. My taste changes constantly, and so does my mental queue of knitting projects that I'm excited to cast on.

Knitting, for me, is mostly about joy. Sometimes it's about doing for others, or making myself something cute to wear. But it is, most fundamentally, a source of pleasure in the doing of it in this moment. I don't want to knit a project, or a yarn, that once was exciting but now feels like eating my vegetables.

Of course, I also don't want to throw away perfectly good yarn, or even give away large amounts of it on a regular basis; yarn is money, in a very direct way. So, over time, I've learned to rein in the acquisitive impulse or, more precisely, redirect that impulse to acquiring yarns that I love right now, and that I'm going to knit right now. I resist forming emotional attachments to yarns of the past.

These days, I never buy a yarn with the intent of stashing it. Owning yarn is no longer a goal or a pleasure in itself. I keep my eyes on the prize, and the prize is to be happy with what I'm knitting right now, in the present.

It works like this. The rule: Buy yarn only if I intend to cast on a project in that yarn right away. What's going on in my brain: I really want to buy this yarn. It's special, and the lighting here in the Marriott Marquis Hotel is so awful that if a yarn looks good here, it must look *amazing* in natural light. Result: I buy the yarn, and to remain in compliance with my no-stashing rule, I cast it on immediately. I now have a half-dozen projects on the needles at all times. How do you like them apples, No-Stashing Rule? I fixed you!

The heart's desire will find a way to game every system, which is why, each year, I donate yarn to a local group that collects and distributes materials to art teachers. I get thank-you notes from teachers, which I read and enjoy (but get rid of immediately). And for a few weeks, I get to feel like a minimalist.

LIBRARY OF WOOL

BY RACHEL ATKINSON

With thanks to Felicity "knitsonik" Ford for the inspiration.

Imagine. A Library of Wool. Wouldn't that be marvelous?

Would it have its own Dewey Decimal System—a "Ewey" System if you please—making each specific breed, weight, and mill easy to put your finger on? Is it purely a research library or would "readers" be allowed to check a skein out? Can anyone visit or do you have to be a patron of the wool world to qualify for admittance, and what credentials would you need to show?

In my Library of Wool dreams there is a beautiful, handcrafted, wooden shelving system (cedar, of course) with perfectly perfect cubbyholes for each individual skein. A metal tag with the shelf reference number stamped into it indicates the yarn is in its right or wrong place. On an ancient oak table in the center of a high-ceilinged room awash with natural light, a box contains index cards—one for each cataloged skein. On the card is a snippet of the yarn and a small swatch with every detail of how it was created. I can take down a skein from the library shelves and sit for hours at the desk taking in the feel, weight, loft, twist, and all manner of finer details about it while seeing how it transforms and blooms once knitted and blocked. I breathe in the scent of the flock and the fields, and with a magnifying glass I look at the plies, seeing how the fibers have been aligned during the spinning process, sensing the terroir as you would a fine wine, and beginning to form an image of the land and the sheep from whence it came.

As the daughter of a shepherd, I grew up surrounded by wool—mainly wool still on the back of sheep, but wool nonetheless. Dad's sheep story began as a hobby with a small flock of Suffolks purchased to train Beth, his first Border Collie sheepdog. We lived in a house on a newbuild estate in North Yorkshire, so Dad rented fields for the sheep to graze on. He would spend evenings with Beth and the sheep, and on weekends we would head off as a family to "One Man and His Dog" trials across the north of England and beyond. Every weekend and holiday was about the soon-multiple dogs and the ever-increasing flock of sheep.

We learned all about sheep and their entire life cycle, from birth to death and everything in between. Spotting ewes in labor was my specialty, and lambing a sheep became Mum's party trick. Spring brought at least one orphan lamb home to live with us, graduating from a cardboard box in the kitchen to a pen in the garden before returning to the field and its flock. My sister and I appear in a series of photographs with a lamb on a lead who became a permanently adopted member of the family. Susie, as we named her, traveled between our back garden and the local farm, where she went to hang out for the day with a pony and a goat. She would be standing by the gate waiting for us to pick her up after school. She'd hop into the front seat of Mum's Mini, and off we'd go back home. She eventually went to live with friends who had a rambling farmhouse in the Yorkshire Dales, where she happily lived out her days with a grumpy goose for company.

You could rest assured the sheep would escape their grassy enclosure at the most inappropriate time, usually just as Mum and Dad were heading out on a Saturday night or as we sat down to Christmas dinner. We ate lamb exclusively for our Sunday lunch; it would be years before we sat down to a roast beef dinner. Somewhere there is a reel of cine-camera footage taken by Mum of me and my sister hanging out with the flock while Dad rides Charlie the big Suffolk ram around the field. They were good times, though a prelude to an acrimonious divorce, after which Mum never cooked lamb again.

Not until years later did I realize how being this close to sheep during those formative years left a permanent mark, an invisible woolly tattoo, on me.

I don't recall shearing days and have no idea what happened to the fleece once shorn, but I do remember Mum cursing over an Aran-style sweater that she knit for Dad from one of the fleeces. It had been spun by a lady in the Yorkshire Dales, more than likely the wife of a sheep farmer Dad would have had dealings with, and was so full of lanolin that Mum struggled to knit it. The stubborn and sticky yarn had to be forced onto the needles, each stitch an overexaggerated movement from one needle to the other and back again. When finally finished, the cursed sweater was so heavy and stiff that I think Dad wore it once before hiding it in the back of the wardrobe. Needless to say, I never saw a skein of yarn from the Suffolks again, or any of Dad's other sheep for that matter, until I began my own yarn journey.

Mum was always knitting, and I would often go with her to the local yarn store to pick out supplies for a new project. This was probably where I first heard the term *stash*.

"I'll see what I've got in my stash."

"I'll stash it until I find the right pattern."

"One more ball won't make a difference to the stash."

Having knitted from early childhood until I was a teenager, I then laid down the needles in favor of books, drawing, and music while indulging my dreams of going to Central Saint Martins to train as a fashion designer. That dream came true, and at the end of four fashion years I was spat out into a world I had no interest in being a part of, before drifting into bookselling and forming my next dream of becoming an illustrated children's book publisher. That one never happened, and, as we know, life tends to take you on its own course. We are often best to follow it and see where it leads.

Just over a decade ago I picked up those needles again and, in between trying to learn every single knitting technique ever invented as quickly as possible, I also began building my own personal stash. What started as a basket by the side of the sofa quickly became a plastic container, which soon became two, three, and four, with an underbed vacuum-sealed storage bag and finally an entire cupboard—my own personal Yarn Library. The stash became a part of me and was top of the "things to consider" list whenever my beloved Mr K and I moved from one rented apartment to another, accompanied by his reassuring words: "Don't get rid of it."

"But I might never knit it," I'd reply.

"But you might."

There have been times when I pondered a radical overhaul of it, something along the lines of Kay-Gardiner-meets-Marie-Kondo. But every time I started unpacking the stash I rediscovered all the treasures therein and just couldn't do it. My stash is so much more than a collection of random yarn. Years of (mainly) discerning purchases—some considered, others impulse buys—have come together to reflect not only my yarn taste and crafting history but also a timeline of how trends and fashions within yarn purchasing have changed over the last ten years.

Inside the Library you will find genuine yarn treasure. A bundle of what must now surely be classed as vintage Rowan tweeds, including a selection of stunning British wool yarns spun in Scotland during its golden days of production. Fox, Chunky, and Harris Tweeds are some of the best tweed yarns I have ever seen and of a type of yarn many

---

My stash is so much more than a collection of random yarn. Years of (mainly) discerning purchases—some considered, others impulse buys—have come together to reflect not only my yarn taste and crafting history but also a timeline of how trends and fashions within yarn purchasing have changed over the last ten years.

modern companies aspire to replicate. Every now and then I have a look at them and contemplate their future, before archiving them once more, safe in the knowledge that they are there for future reference.

A plethora of multicolored sock yarns from the one-skein wonders department dominates the Library, and I can date most of them to a very specific time and place in my yarn purchasing. Many represent defunct indie companies, and some of the most treasured skeins are a testament to the skills of yarn dyers we may never again see in action.

My deep love of a good mohair or bouclé yarn (a hangover from the 1980s) occupies a corner of the Library with contemporary inter-pretations by modern dyers and spinners. These yarns rub shoulders with a few novelty relics from the 1980s: Pingouin, Bouton d'Or, and a number of other French companies whose knitting and crochet style was so influential during that decade. Will I ever use these yarns? Who knows. What I *do* know is that they are close at hand.

In September 2015, I embarked on a project that would change my outlook not only on yarn but also on the entire wool industry and—I can even go so far as to say—on my life. This project has influenced a rapidly growing section of my Library. First, a little background story . . .

Eventually, Dad turned his hobby into his full-time occupation. He now works as a shepherd for a country estate in North Yorkshire looking after the Escrick Park Estate Hebridean sheep alongside his own Hebridean flock. They are a hardy and primitive breed of horned sheep, small and elegant, with deep brown, almost black, fleeces that become tinted in the sun and fade to gray with age. They are predomi-nantly used for conservation grazing, working their way through the estate woodland, nibbling away unwanted trees, shrubs, and grasses, thus enabling many other plants and animals to thrive.

Looking at the sheep with a knitter's eyes, I would dream of work-ing with the beautiful, naturally dark fleece from their backs—an entire lifetime of stash was right there in front of me. I wondered if it was time to dust off the spindle and practice spinning again. Then I remembered why I hadn't continued my spinning adventures: I feared that another stash would take over our home. Besides, why DIY when you can employ people who are masters of this fine art to do it for you?

Sadly, these amazing fleeces were considered pretty much worthless by the British Wool Marketing Board. Dad received a payment that equated to 3 pence—that's £0.03—per fleece. The 2015 clip was sitting in a barn, the occasional fleece being taken out and used for protecting a tree or plugging a gap in the hedgerow. Outrageous! It got me thinking, *What if I did something with the wool instead?* A trip to the Swedish island of Gotland sealed the deal: Having seen the beautiful, silvery, native sheep grazing alongside a farm store selling their processed and spun fleece as finished yarn, I knew I had to give it a go. It makes sense, doesn't it? Here are the sheep, here is the fleece, here is the yarn. So simple and yet something so many knitters, crocheters, and yarn crafters lose sight of. Many simply never have the opportunity to connect the dots.

Fueled with determination and a sense of "this is something I have to do," I emptied my piggy bank of its house down payment and took a leap into the unknown, trusting that the fleece would be a viable raw product to spin into yarn. I had no idea if people would get it or indeed get behind it. Would the yarn be coarse and unwieldy? Would it be good for anything at all? But it worked, by golly, it worked, and people did get it, and they got behind it, and these little sheep propelled me into unknown territory. Starting with the resulting yarn from the Hebrideans, I rapidly began to build my Library of Wool and put the skeins into circulation under the Daughter of a Shepherd label.

I developed a deep thirst for information about natural wools from all corners of the world, along with the breeds of sheep that produce them, the mills that spin them, and the knowledgeable/visionary people and brave adventurers who have also taken steps into the world of wool. As my learning journey continues, a huge influx of acquisitions—additional reference volumes if you like—have been entered into both my Library of Wool and my Library of Books.

What do we use libraries for? To read, learn, and research, and in doing so we discover new words:

- *Staple*
- *Crimp*
- *Cotted*
- *Dags*
- *Kemp*

Even my beloved can now tell the difference between woolen-spun and worsted-spun yarns. We are all always learning and will continue to do so. It is the fuel that keeps us going, and libraries are the gateway to this knowledge.

But it doesn't stop there. A new dream has formed: of one day building a Living Library of Wool. Every now and then you will see or hear about people who have a motley crew of sheep, with just a few examples of different breeds coming together to make a larger flock. They might have a handful of rare breeds, orphans, or simply random sheep gathered to maintain the lawn, but the opportunity to be up close with these incredible beasts leads to a deeper understanding of where our yarn comes from, how sensitive it is to its surroundings, and the number of hours it actually takes to raise a sheep that will produce enough fleece to spin into a usable end product. These sheep are living proof of the true value of the wool we so often take for granted.

Speaking of which, Dad just called to tell me he was on his way to pick up the latest addition to his own Living Library of Wool—and, along with it, a new project for me to tackle. And so, 'twas ever thus.

HER PRETTY STRING
BY FRANKLIN HABIT

I was seven years old when the lust for pretty string drove me to an act of larceny.

While my parents slept, I crept into the closet where my mother kept her craft supplies and took the following:

- one sewing needle
- two sheets of graph paper
- one leftover scrap of even-weave Aida cloth, about the size of my hand
- four partial skeins of silk embroidery floss in russet brown, pink, bright blue, and grass green
- one spool of black polyester thread
- one spool of red polyester thread

These I placed inside a Buster Brown shoebox given to me to house my baseball card collection. As I had only two baseball cards, there was plenty of room. I hid the shoebox in the deepest recesses of the gloom under my bed.

My first stash was thus built on a foundation of stolen goods. It was naughty of me, but I was desperate. I wasn't supposed to touch those things. I wasn't supposed to want them.

Toy soldiers were showered upon me in abundance. Bats and rackets and balls of all varieties were pressed into my hands. I was offered my choice of shiny pocketknives, urged to play with kits that started fires, tempted with the offer of a BB gun. The grown-ups who ruled my world were quite clear. They hoped very much that I would be inclined to throw, kick, hit, stab, burn, and shoot stuff like a "normal" boy.

But all I really wanted to do was play with pretty string.

My pilfered stash was well on its way to becoming a tiny cross-stitched picture of a brown rabbit sitting on a pink-and-blue Easter egg when my mother caught me in the act of backstitching. She blew her stack. Not only had I stolen from her, but also—and this was the greater crime—I was Acting Like a Girl.

You may have learned to knit, sew, or crochet at your mother's knee. My mother used that knee to nudge me away. She was restless by nature, only truly content when her hands were occupied. I inherited the restlessness and wanted to do as she did, but pleas for a lesson or at least a closer look were firmly (sometimes violently) discouraged. "How many times do I have to say it? This is not for you. This is for girls."

I hated that. Sometimes I hated her. She was cruel, I thought, to sit in front of me smugly turning out embroidery and afghans and even the clothes on my back but refusing to share the secrets of how any of it was done. I can see now that she said "This is not for you" with a certain desperation, biting her tongue. She would have taught me everything, I think, had she not believed it was in my best interest to stay on the narrow path of American masculinity. The world was, and is, horribly cruel to boys who don't act like boys.

But years of forceful shepherding by a strong woman couldn't keep me from making my way to yarn. After learning the rudiments of knitting from a college classmate, my next stop was the fusty needlework shop in Harvard Square. When I was met with a blunt "This is not for you" from the prissy owner, I found that a decade of fighting with Mom had taught me to say, "Yes, it is."

As my passion for knitting grew, I stashed yarns the way a nouveau-riche billionaire collects art: rapidly, and with more enthusiasm than taste. I bought stout American wools from small American mills.

I bought rich, exuberant colors from the emerging community of hand-dyers. I bought fine silk blends and dreamy imported alpaca. I also bought "rustic" farmers' market wools so rough they wore a hole in the bottom of my shopping bag and cheap, gaudy Chinese acrylics that squeaked across my needles like angry mice. It was all yarn to me, and I wanted all the yarn.

I didn't tell my mother.

I was in my mid-thirties and becoming a semiprofessional knitter by the time she worked up the nerve to ask about the basket of yarn next to the couch, the basket of yarn next to the bed, the overstuffed glass-fronted cabinet of yarn in the dining room, and the Saxony spinning wheel that had displaced the coffee table.

"So," Mom said. "You're really getting into this knitting."

"Yep," I said.

"I used to crochet a lot," she said.

"I remember," I said.

Another year passed.

We gathered at my sister's house for Christmas. About half the gifts I gave that year were knitted; a few had been chronicled on my burgeoning knitting blog. My mother discovered the blog and figured out how to leave a comment on a picture of a wrap in progress. It said, "That is looking great."

I was so thrilled, I called her to say thank you.

"A lot of people like your knitting," she said.

"I guess so," I said.

"I'm surprised," she said.

As my passion for knitting grew, I stashed yarns the way a nouveau-riche billionaire collects art: rapidly, and with more enthusiasm than taste.

On Christmas morning, as my sister snuggled into her new wrap, I opened a box with a tag that said FROM MOM AND DAD to find a Meg Swansen video and a bundle of knitting notions from Schoolhouse Press.

I was speechless.

"I called and asked to make sure these were things you could use," Mom said. "They were real nice on the phone."

"Thank you," I said. "This is just perfect."

"We should go to a yarn store," she said. "I want you to teach me how to knit."

"I'd love to," I said.

She took to knitting the way she took to every sort of handwork she touched: from novice to master in a matter of months. And she began, of course, to amass a stash of her own. First a basket, then two baskets, then a colony of large plastic bins in the closet in the guest room.

Her friends began to ask if she would give lessons. With characteristic frankness she agreed, provided they supplied their own yarn.

"I'm not giving you my good stuff," she said. "And if you want to knit with crap, that's up to you."

Then I posted a picture on my blog of a single quilt block I had pieced by hand just to see if I could do it.

"That looks fun," she said. "Next time you visit, I want you to go with me to this cute little fabric place that opened near us. I think I might like to make a quilt."

Six months later she started leading block-of-the-month classes and splurged on a fancy new sewing machine. The yarn stash disappeared under sedimentary layers of Kona cottons and batting. The guest room became the sewing room, and when I visited I had to sleep on an air mattress wedged between the cutting table and the design wall. If I snored too much, I woke up covered in half-square triangles.

She began to measure various spaces with an eye to parking a longarm quilting machine on the premises.

"I love quilting," she said. "I just love it."

For her sixty-third birthday, I sent her a bundle of fat quarter fabrics for her stash and a bunch of flowers. My father's gift was the promise of a vacation in Hawaii to visit old friends and escape the gray Midwestern winter. On the fourth day of the trip, the flood of happy snapshots showing Mom by the pool, on the balcony, and on the beach suddenly stopped. I assumed they'd drifted into a state of disconnected island bliss and felt happy for them.

Then I got a call. It was my father, with an uncharacteristic tremble in his voice. After a few days of feeling a bit queasy, my mother had collapsed on the street. The whites of her eyes were yellow. She'd been taken from the emergency room to Tripler Army Medical Center for surgery on her pancreas.

We made hurried arrangements to get her home. About a week later came the diagnosis: cancer. Cancer in her pancreas. Cancer in her liver. She fought an ugly, painful fight and left us a year to the day after the flight to Honolulu.

The night she died we were all in the house, but only my father was beside her. I was downstairs in the sewing room, tossing and turning on that air mattress wedged between the cutting table and the design wall. There were unfinished projects everywhere. The pieces of her latest quilt were stacked near the sewing machine: finished blocks to the left, unfinished to the right. One square in midseam still under the presser foot.

My father broke the news. I went up to say good-bye. While I held her cold hand, I thought about our last conversation.

She had seen my newest design for *Vogue Knitting* magazine and thought it was beautiful—but not something she would ever wear. Too fancy. Still, she was impressed. She loved the Elizabeth Zimmermann Moebius scarf I had made for her, at her request, with a combination of fingering-weight cashmere, silk, Merino, and alpaca yarns mixed together.

"It's so light and soft," she'd said. Her booming contralto voice was in shreds by then; she sounded like a tattered blanket flapping in the wind. "And so pretty. You know my colors. It fits just right. The nurses all loved it. I told them, 'Yeah, my son made it.'"

I'd talked about a current project, a crocheted rug, that was giving me fits. I'd tried to make her laugh. She had. Then she said she needed to rest. That was that.

I don't know how long I knelt there holding her hand. Other people drifted in and out. My sister told me gently that the undertakers were coming. She knew I couldn't bear the thought of watching as our mother's body was carted away. I went back to the sewing room and closed the door.

Upstairs, she was gone. Downstairs, she was everywhere. Her perfume lingered. Her hands had arranged everything, and during our two weeks' vigil I had been almost superstitiously careful not to touch anything. The obedient son, or at least nearly so, to the end.

All her things are here, I whispered, *so she must still be here. This is her yellow pincushion.*

I stumbled around the room, whispering to myself.

Here is her spool rack. This is where she keeps the rulers. The pens and pencils go in that cup. This is her rotary cutter, and these are the good scissors that we only use for fabric. These are the scissors for paper. Finished blocks go here. Unfinished blocks go there. This is her iron. This is her serger. She hasn't started sewing this quilt yet because she thinks it might need more red.

I opened the closet, and there were the shelves with their full bins of cotton and one familiar wicker basket. I opened it. Half a scarf: cream, cashmere, moss stitch, on the needles.

She was still there.

The working world does not observe mourning. Within a week I was on an airplane heading for the Pacific Northwest to teach at a fiber festival. In the month that followed, I was at home for six scattered days. The month after that, for eight. The month after that, for five. Articles were due. Patterns were due. Cartoons and photographs were due. "We know you must be sad," said the emails, "but we want to make sure you're on target." Life, as they say, goes on. Deadlines do, anyhow.

I checked in with my father as often as I could.

"Your sister is going to go through the clothes and shoes," he said when I called from an airport in Florida. "I don't know about the sewing room, though. I don't know what anything is for."

"Leave that to me," I said. "I'll help you. Just close the door. Please don't give anything away until I have a chance to sort things out."

"Okay," he said. "Come as soon as you can."

He tried to wait, but the closed door tormented him. By the time I arrived, the sewing room was a guest room again.

He was proud of it. The polished wooden top of the cutting table, which he had built for her as a present, was still there—now as the headboard of the new bed. "I wanted to keep a part of Momma in here," he said. "I miss her so much." It was a beautiful tribute.

I could only see what wasn't there. The sewing table, gone. The design wall, gone. The pegboard festooned with dozens of rulers, gone. I opened cabinet doors and drawers. Empty. I opened the closet. Empty.

It smelled very clean. The gentle scent of her perfume had vanished.

"There's still one basket of knitting stuff," said my father. "I'd like you to sort that out for me."

His voice sounded very far away. My pulse was throbbing in my ears. Where were her things?

I said, "It looks great, Pop."

I thought, *Where is my mother?*

Death takes an instant, but the dead leave you bit by bit. Walking into the room, I knew she was gone. Looking around, for the first time I felt it.

My father, good as his word, hadn't scattered everything to the wind. The fabric was with my mother's friend Dollie, a fellow quilter and a great comfort in her last year. That was as it should be. For me, he had saved the rest.

I dug through the boxes in the basket and pulled out memories: her favorite shears, the yellow pincushion, notebooks half-filled with her loopy writing, the well-worn metal seam guide she had used to alter my school uniforms. Remarkably, almost impossibly, her entire perfectly organized collection of embroidery floss was still intact, the same stash I had plundered thirty-odd years before. Crowning it all, my father decided that I should inherit her fancy sewing machine.

The machine is here in my workroom, still in the case. I haven't opened it yet. It's as complicated and imposing as she was. I wish she were here. I wish she would teach me what to do with all this pretty string.

MOVING YARN / PORTABLE STORIES
BY ANNA MALTZ

When I lived in San Francisco for five years, like any responsible local, I had an earthquake kit containing essentials to tide me over if I survived when the worst happened: bottled water, tinned food (and an opener), matches, blankets, and a flashlight. When I travel, I carry a small first aid kit with plasters for blisters and cuts, pills for headaches and acid stomachs, and creams for bruises and burns. I can always find folding scissors, a safety pin, tissues, and a sanitary towel in my purse (regardless of what time of the month it is). My freezer is well stocked with frozen peas, pasta sauce, ice cubes, and cake. Likewise, I have a healthy yarn stash and I am never far from a knitting project in progress. I like to be prepared for all sorts of eventualities, good and bad.

In a similar vein, I keep a list of topics I might like to write a dissertation on, just in case I ever decide I am truly that way inclined. "Why we stash" is on there. I'm intrigued by the basic humanity of crafters' attachment to materials and tools, to the raw materials of creativity, entertainment, and making things. There is a deep optimism in how much we acquire and keep around, and in our belief that we can make and learn from that vast quantity in a single lifetime. Thinking historically, a stash is a bit of an itchy ghost limb of the recent past, which includes wartime rationing of materials and food, a real scarcity that hasn't been experienced on that scale in the West for years. Working backward, we are not too many generations away from a time before industrialization, when making by hand was the only choice and when having the resources to do so was a distinct benefit. The volume at which things can now enter the world is a novelty on the evolutionary scale.

In my experience, storing things with potential and possibility is so much a part of creative territory. Creativity is all about being resourceful, about using things at hand and even making something from nothing. Yarn is both something and nothing. It is very much yarn—but its purpose is to become something else. In a way, yarn isn't something until it has been knitted, either into a garment or perhaps a less-wearable object with less-tangible function.

When I consider why we—why I—stash, I start by thinking of a stash at its most basic: as a collection. Collecting is an intrinsically human activity. It's both hunting and gathering. Like other human activities, it comes with hierarchies and questions of privilege.

For as long as anyone who knows me can remember, I have been a collector. I've been the creator of fleeting collections of frogs, lady-bugs, and seeds in gardens and parks. Permanent ones like stickers; erasers; novelty soaps; stamps; Fimo modeling clay; figurines of pigs, owls, and armadillos; 5-pence pieces; lost marbles . . . Even as an adult, my pockets still need careful checking for found treasures before they are put in the wash. I love collections of items. Once I have a couple of something, it feels like the start of a beautiful collection. It's as if these "somethings" have found each other and are now ready to add babies and friends to build a bigger, stronger community.

When I consider why we—why I—stash, I start by thinking of a stash at its most basic: as a collection. Collecting is an intrinsically human activity. It's both hunting and gathering. Like other human activities, it comes with hierarchies and questions of privilege.

As I've grown up I've learned that not all collections are created equal. There are acceptable things to collect and those that are less so. Different types of collections impart different types of assumptions about the character of the collector. Books facilitate an air of intelligence; records suggest passion and engagement; art endows the owner with the appearance of culture, taste, and wealth; fast cars disguise a small willy; shoes purport to a healthy social life or excess body weight. It's been my experience that a bountiful yarn stash is perceived as a distinct indication you are slightly nutty and lack restraint.

When people see my yarn collection, they raise eyebrows and make comments. At home, we have *a lot* of books, but no one says anything disparaging about them. At most we are asked whether we have read them all. Unlike yarn, books are a common and condoned thing to collect. The world is full of book collections: in homes, libraries, offices, hotels, you name it. There are also many books on collecting. Some cover preexisting collections, such as those held in museums and by fancy individuals. Others advise on how to approach collecting everything from art to seeds and even friends. Some help value and catalog specific collections for enthusiasts of items such as buttons, baseball cards, pottery, fossils, and zippers. Interior design books explore how to make your collections look just so, and scientific tomes outline how to safely store and preserve your collections. Even philosophical books exist on the sociology, anatomy, and psychology of collecting. I have a couple of those. They are some of my favorite books I haven't read. On the flip side, you can find self-help books on how to rid yourself of your collections, along with the other shackles that bind. Clearly the act of collecting is an integral part of the human experience, and it is affected by both permanence and transience.

Before we moved into our flat, we spent a year being itinerant in my native city of London. I guess, technically, we were homeless. Thankfully, we weren't anywhere near sleeping rough, but we didn't have our own address and weren't in a position to get one. We housesat a string of very grown-up abodes belonging to friends of my parents. Each place followed the next like clockwork until they didn't, and then we sublet from a friend of a friend, an actor who was headed to LA to try his luck in pilot season. The short-term rental was arranged the day he flew out, so everything was as he left it, with pictures of his children on the bedside table and dirty laundry in the hamper. The whole year offered us an amazing insight into how other people live in their spaces. (We were only partially their guests, because they weren't around at the time, but it wasn't as if we were in our own home.) This unprecedented view into other people's lives gave us a distinct opportunity to reflect on what we found important in our *own* lives.

As we house-hopped, moving every two weeks to three months, we transported our essentials by borrowing my parents' car. Beyond clothes and my own pillow, I brought my knitting gear. Four large boxes contained a pared-down selection of yarn from my stash, plus notions and needles. Having handknitted since I was five, I had recently added machine knitting to my skill set and was keen to practice. For that reason, a Brother KH910 and collapsible table got lugged along, too. While we could rely on the fact that each house we stayed in would have pots, pans, bedding, and towels we could borrow, I knew that none had a ball winder or a swift. I was happy to store my books for a year, knowing I could revisit them later, borrow them from friends or a library, or, in a total emergency, track down a copy online. My stash and tools don't work that way, so they traveled with me.

It certainly wasn't ideal to move so often and with so much stuff. But it also wasn't terrible. It was an interesting education. We'll probably never live in houses that size again, and we certainly won't own them. Finally, we started renting our own tiny flat. As soon as we moved into what initially looked like an empty white shoebox with a sink and washing machine at one end, we lined a whole wall with flatpack bookshelves. As we unpacked our library into its new home, it became our home. Art, philosophy, cocktails, and cookbooks, with a few novels thrown in for good measure. It was good to see them again after a year in storage. We have more books at the studio (a space that we started renting a few months later, because two creative practices weren't fitting in a one-bedroom). My studio bookshelves house mostly knitting-related instructional and inspirational books and pamphlets. Other textile and craft techniques get spots, too, as well as books on animals and flowers. The rest of the space is for yarn, fabric, assorted haberdashery, and old artworks.

My stash is both a diary and a sketchbook, not stored in words and pictures but in color and texture. I have rarely bought yarn without having a plan for what it would become. Seeing it again triggers a mental catalog of ideas. That may not be what it eventually becomes. Rather, it's a sketch, a rough idea. What yarn *becomes* can change. Even after it has been knitted, it can be undone. Once it has been knitted, it carries with it additional memories. The diary of its creation gets written as you go along, augmented by the adventures and trials and tribulations encountered as it is being worn. Words aren't the only way to record such things, though they may be an easier way to share them.

Anyone can read words, but the story of a ball, skein, and oddment is a personal one. Each is a reminder of the moment I acquired the yarn. Mid-teenage Anna ordering dark chocolate brown mohair over the phone to make my bestie a cardigan, the matronly Northern accent on the other end of the line using a word I'd never use to describe that color (or anything else, for that matter). I ended my teens avoiding the sharp elbows of frantic older ladies in the post-Christmas sale bins. I held my own doing battle for marked-down bags of Jaeger and

My stash is both a diary and a sketchbook, not stored in words and pictures but in color and texture.

Rowan DK. At the other end of the market was the treasure-hunting thrill of finding a jumper's worth of vintage peach mercerized cotton 4-ply under a pile of musty striped curtains in a charity shop basket.

By my early twenties, knitting had become the center of my art practice. With the aid of the yellow pages, I phoned around the country to track down Superman yellow mohair when it was super out of fashion. The Internet was in its infancy, and I had just come up with my first wacky Hotmail address. Back then, it wasn't yet obvious how to track down a color that looked like nipples without having to voice the question to someone over the phone.

A couple of years later, during my postgraduate fine art studies, I had the tough decision of whether to blow my budget on Chroma Key Blue angora to reconstitute an invisible giant bunny. By now I was able to trawl through janky French websites that assured me no rabbits were harmed in the making. Soon I discovered the bright colors of Lamb's Pride while witnessing the tentative reappearance of local yarn shops in the San Francisco Bay Area. That was in my mid-twenties, and those colors were so refreshing after the washed-out death tones and closing wool shops of the United Kingdom in the nineties. Suddenly I was visibly not the only under-fifty person knitting. These skeins and balls are scrapbooks of my travels, of finding time-warped yarn shops in far-flung cities. Increasingly, they are reminders of in-depth conversations with independent dyers and spinners, friends all.

I readily admit that I am not a minimalist. I find solace in the fact that the traditional Japanese minimal aesthetic was made possible by the equally traditional *kura* (storehouse) where the items not in use or on display in the home would be kept. I like being surrounded by things that inspire me and allow me to start new projects instantly.

I know it's wrong, but I do judge people. An obsession with minimalism has always smacked to me of a romanticism of poverty (and potentially an outdated one at that) from a wealthy perspective. I think of Marie Antoinette having a little farm built on the castle grounds so that she could play at being a peasant shepherdess. Considered minimalism in this day and age is generally a pastime for those with the affluence to buy (or rebuy) what they need, when they need it. The considered minimalist needn't be as resourceful about keeping things around "just in case," because, at any moment, he or she can replenish the shelves with abundance.

Of course, there are extremes to acquiring and keeping things around. I am not advocating hoarding. I think of fashion icon Iris Apfel's clothing collection—how amazing, over the top, obsessive, and opulent it is. While the volume of her acquisitions is phenomenal and indeed excessive, I think of all the designers she has supported via her purchases over the years. There is something hugely important in that. In parallel, by purchasing yarn, we are often supporting the creative practices of people we believe in and connect to as individuals and/ or by what they produce. These small businesses and independents are, for the most part, not making the world worse. In fact, they are headed in the right direction, which stops me from saying, "Let's stop buying new stuff and use what there is," even though that's probably what should happen. So much already exists in the world. The onus should be on *not* acquiring, rather than on throwing away or "letting go" to make way for more new things.

When it comes to too much stuff, there are definite degrees of "yuck." As a teenager, a friend of mine finally cleared up the piles of clothing and study books in her room, only to discover a few moldy takeaway boxes under the bed growing beautiful pastel-colored forests of fuzz. My sister briefly worked for a family who had gone through a trauma and had a room in the house where unsorted laundry and unopened purchases went. It was also the room the dog used as a toilet, because no one could cope with letting it out.

I console myself that I'm not in that category. I do have too much yarn (and other things), but it's the right kind of good shit, and I'm not quite sure how to quantify it. It's certainly more than those four (or was it six?) boxes I carried from place to place the year we were drifters. If separated out from my other belongings, I'd say it could easily fill a walk-in closet or maybe Van Gogh's *Bedroom in Arles,* as he painted it in 1889, if I haven't misread the perspective. I've heard knitters say they have more yarn than they could knit in a lifetime. It's referred to as reaching SABLE—Stash Acquisition Beyond Life Expectancy. Happily this is not the case for me. The quantity I have is both inspirational and overwhelming enough.

As a medium-fast knitter, I estimate I could work my way through my current stash in about a decade; half that if I used my knitting machine for the majority of it. Of course it would depend on what I was knitting, and no *new* yarn could be added to my stash. I'm not an avid consumer, so I could fairly easily have a personal moratorium on yarn buying. Lately I find it easier not to buy new things than to part with what I have, especially if just to make way for new things.

There is a stigma to making do. Even in the resourceful, creative world of knitting, we are constantly being pushed to experience the excitement of owning something new. I'm not oblivious to that excitement, but I get to satisfy my itch for new things using the yarns that pass my way for collaborative projects, for work. If I am writing a pattern and knitting up the sample, it is standard to do it in a repeatable yarn that anyone can buy—and not just a type and brand of yarn but the specific color. (Some people like to be exact like that.) It makes advertising sense to use currently available yarn rather than encouraging people to use what they already have stashed. My work lets me experience these new yarns. I even get to try on the resulting garments, though they are not mine to wear. But I'm still left with a lot of stashed yarn I feel a tad guilty about not using. There's only so much one woman can knit.

Which brings us to the real question. Do I *have* to knit all of my yarn? Ever? We've read many of the books in our collection, some even from cover to cover. And we also have yet to read a lot of them. In fact, some of my favorite books are ones I haven't read yet. Before reading a book, it is open to all my fantasies of the wonderful tales and answers it will contain. It is everything I want it to be. The possibilities are endless. But the moment I read it, the book becomes what it is, anchored by the words as they intentionally appear on the page and by my interpretation of them. Until then, they can be whatever I want them to be—a little like yarn before it becomes a knit. I feel about my yarn stash as I do about my library: It is the record of much of my history, promise, potential, inspiration, learning, and space to dream. I won't read every book I own, and I won't knit every centimeter of yarn—and some of it is better that way.

FEAR NOT

BY SUE SHANKLE

Does the size and magnitude of your stash strike fear in you? Do you worry about yourself? Do your loved ones give you a hard time about that stash?

Fear not. I am here to help.

I am a clinical social worker. No, I don't walk into random homes wearing a seafoam green polyester pantsuit and take unsuspecting people's children away from them. That is a stereotype I will fight to dispel until the end of days. I am a mental health clinician. I am trained to assess, diagnose, and treat mental disorders. I help people figure out how to solve problems, traverse mammoth systems, and, hopefully, feel better. I have worked with lots of different kinds of people with lots of diagnoses.

I am also a knitter with a stash that seems to multiply while I sleep. I am not complaining.

The term *stash* meant something entirely different when I was a young, bell bottom–clad person. Maybe it still does; I have no way of knowing. But today, loosely defined, a *yarn stash* is whatever one keeps around the house in case the urge descends. You bought it because you liked it.

Let's get this out in the open right away: I do not think having a big ol' curated stash is a problem. There might be those who do. Problem identification is an excellent coping skill that works in many situations. But if someone dislikes my stash, that is not *my* problem. See how easy that is? I have a friend who likes shoes. She keeps them on hand because one never knows when one will be inspired to show off. Can yarn be much different?

I began knitting after an accident left me bedridden and really mad about it. The Internet had just become a regular daily thing, so my stash began with eBay mistakes—like cones of chenille. Fortunately, I learn quickly. That morphed into buying yarn while on vacation or heading for the LYS when I've had a particularly hard day. When I started, I had no idea that I would learn so much about sheep, people who love them, and myself.

I still occasionally make Internet purchases. Thanks to those kind ones who work hard to research and educate us (you know who you are), we can all now make excellent choices based on the excellent work of our peers.

So, buying yarn is a regular thing for me. I buy yarn with no project in mind. My knitting is yarn-driven. I can rationalize this.

I am educated about defense mechanisms, like denial (overused), projection (my personal favorite), and rationalization. For our purposes and so as not to be boring, let's define rationalization simply as the way one justifies behavior. Here's my rationalization: At various times throughout the year, I will spend money on entertainment and gifts for loved ones. Contributing to my stash ensures I will have what I need, when I need it, for less than the cost of a movie per week or gift certificates for people who deserve better.

And really, does anybody believe that Michelangelo just decided to carve the *David* one day and went out and bought a slab of marble? Heck no. He had that thing sitting around for a long time before he even started. Because he had to look at it, play with it, and possibly sniff it before he started to work. He planned that stuff. That's what we artists do.

My stash is my inspiration. I like looking at it and remembering what a great time I was having when I bought it. Buying yarn on vacation is the best. It's easy to smoosh into an overpacked suitcase, it doesn't weigh much, and it's guaranteed to bring back fond memories. I bought some beautiful Missoni wool in a shop in Florence (Italy, not

And really, does anybody believe that Michelangelo just decided to carve the David *one day and went out and bought a slab of marble? Heck no. He had that thing sitting around for a long time before he even started. Because he had to look at it, play with it, and possibly sniff it before he started to work. He planned that stuff. That's what we artists do.*

South Carolina) from a lovely woman who took me out on her balcony overlooking the river to show me her window boxes. Years later, I used some of that to knit Mama a blanket. She likes that blanket. It's warm and it's pretty. I like that she likes it. I like that it keeps her warm. It's the least I can do for her.

When I recently bought a new-to-me home, one of the things I loved the most was the floor-to-ceiling shelves in the laundry room, which also has a door I can close. That and the sunroom had me sold.

My sister helped me move. When she walked into the house carrying two large garbage bags full of yarn, she said, "You need to go to a meeting and get a button."

"You mean a chip? Like AA, only KA?"

"Whatever," she said. "This is ridiculous." There was an eyeroll.

I'm sure it appears that way to nonbelievers. I get it. My sister has no way of understanding, which is fine. She doesn't have to. I still knit stuff for her. She likes it. (I think.)

Many people in my practice spend inordinate amounts of time trying to explain to others "what it's like to be me." It rarely works. People have a hard enough time understanding themselves. Expecting others to "get" you (or your love of beautiful yarn) is not always realistic.

That's why you need a posse. People who understand it all, no explanation necessary. And now we can connect, even in the middle of the night. I have such a group. I am thankful for them all the time. (You know who you are.) Finding my tribe and being a part of it has been a rich experience. It remains that way. So get a posse. Communicate with them whenever you feel misunderstood.

People around you, especially those who share living space with you, may have strong opinions about your stash. It's helpful not to defend said stash, since your loved one may not get it anyway. It really is fine to disagree about it, unless of course your loved one gets nasty. That would be another subject for another day, but one that would require attention.

So if you feel safe enough, help the people around you focus on other things. Help them to understand that living with your yarn is the rent they pay for your company/kickass chicken salad/mad Scrabble skills/whatever you like. Let them enjoy their own special pursuits. Make attempts at appreciating theirs, even if you don't. Being accepting will go a long way when you are on vacation and want to peek into the LYS.

Those are all rationalizations for having a stash with no shame. But some of you might still worry about the size and cost of your stash, as well as your ability to live long enough to knit it all. While I'm not trained to advise on the life-span issues, I can help you work through the worries about stash size and cost.

Start by asking yourself why you have stash anxiety. (Yes, I made that term up. It's not in the *DSM-5*.) Is it because you watched a hoarding show and are now worried about your inability to control yourself? Are others worried about you?

If you are not able to walk through your home or sleep in your bed because of items you couldn't resist buying, you have a problem. If you spend money that you don't have on things that you don't need (common human needs are food, clothing, shelter), then you might have a problem. Seek specific professional help. Hoarding has components in major depressive disorder and obsessive compulsive disorder, and a trusted professional can provide you with some understanding and skills to manage it all.

Anxiety can be harsh and take up conscious brain space. Believe it or not, only 14 percent of brain space is conscious. The rest is not. So if you are anxious, it takes up valuable brain space that would be far better spent on enjoyable pursuits.

I read a recent study that was done with elderly people who have a lot of anxiety because they worry about forgetting things. They end up using brain space for worry, and, sure enough, they forget things. Worry is one thing. Careful consideration is different, and it can be an effective agent for change.

So what bothers you about your stash? If you buy yarn and then feel horrible about it, you're defeating the entire endeavor. There is no shame in loving your stash. None.

If you have stash anxiety, ask yourself two questions, and write down the answers. I regularly recommend my clients make lists. It clears your head and helps you make decisions without fretting.

Question 1: Is your stash manageable? If you think it isn't, write down why. What action(s) would you need to take in order to make it manageable?

So what bothers you about your stash? If you buy yarn and then feel horrible about it, you're defeating the entire endeavor. There is no shame in loving your stash. None.

I am no excellent organizer. I tried storing my stash in plastic tubs that I put up on closet shelves and underneath various beds. What a disaster. I need to be able to see everything so I can find that skein of yak I bought in 2010 without having to pull everything out. Again. Now I use plastic bags, small ones. They are nicely stacked (sort of) on those excellent shelves in the laundry room—and they keep out those nasty moths. I still have a few bags in the hall closet. And the most treasured skeins go in my great-grandmother's cedar chest. I am comfortable with this setup, so my conscious brain space is free to be used for something other than anxiety.

You need your materials near you when creativity strikes. Some days the force is stronger than others. Creativity can show up at any time. As a former Girl Scout, I take the saying "Be prepared" seriously. It has helped many times throughout my life and career.

Question 2: What can you do to make yourself more emotionally comfortable?

Again, write it down. Make a list and get specific. At this stage you may decide to drag it all out, give it a good look, and get rid of the things you know you will never use. Do you need to look at your stash regularly, or not?

Make your list action-based. Separate your feelings from the facts. This is another technique that is helpful in many situations. An example of a fact would be, "I have so much pink yarn." A feeling would be, "I don't like pink yarn."

People get these two mixed up all the time, especially now that newspeople have started to talk about their feelings instead of just stating the facts. A great example of the mix-up would be road rage. Some person in the right lane gets really angry (feeling) when the person in the left lane does not signal when about to change (fact). Sometimes people just need validation that they are really being heard.

I worked myself into a big mad the other day. It was about something I could personally do little to change, but I was indignant. It consumed energy and was a completely worthless way to spend my time. So I got out my pencil and paper (I like pencils, because . . . erasers) and wrote down what I could do to abate it:

1. Wind new yarn.
2. Pet heads of sleeping dogs.
3. Take a long walk through a lovely park.
4. Knit in the sunroom while blaring Steely Dan's "Kid Charlemagne."

Those are things I enjoy, and it worked. Identifying your own such things and having a handy list ready to review can slow down the forward motion of getting worked up.

Hopefully, understanding why you have your stash—and having no shame in loving it—will help you enjoy it even more. Whether others have complete acceptance of your stash is not your problem. When you want to talk about it, seek out those who do understand.

And the really good news? If you decide you need to de-stash, you know where I am.

YARN: A LOVE STORY

BY AMY CHRISTOFFERS

I learned to knit because of a yarn. It was a lavender brushed mohair that had been knitted up into a light, lacy scarf hanging in a shop window. I was in college. I was depressed, I was broke, and I was having a kind of identity crisis.

I was a sophomore in a bachelor of fine arts program, studying painting. Every day we would create something. Then another something. Then we'd have a critique. Then we'd create again. When I wasn't in class I was doing projects for homework. When I wasn't doing homework, I was working. I had two jobs: On weekdays I worked at the school library, where I could also do homework, and on weekends I worked in a jewelry and gift shop, where I could not. Friends were graduating with their BFAs and finding jobs in coffee shops and retail stores. In other words, they had the same jobs we worked while we were in school but with more debt, more rent, and the added cost of health insurance. Art supplies can be expensive. Art takes up space. Where was I going to keep all of this stuff? Who would want it? How was I going to support myself? I was nineteen years old and having a panic attack. So I took a walk.

It was a raw, drizzly, early November day in New England. I started out aimlessly walking down a street I'd walked hundreds of times before. It was just a few blocks from the downtown where the banks, cafés, shops, and diners were; a section of town that was no longer commercial but hadn't become residential yet, either. In a shop window I'd never noticed, a lavender mohair beacon seemed to appear out of nowhere. Suddenly I HAD TO HAVE IT. Without any thought at all, I found myself inside a yarn shop.

The shop was empty except for the owner, who looked as surprised as I was to find me there. But she was friendly enough when she asked how she could help me. I stammered something about the scarf in the window, and she told me that if I wanted it I'd have to make it myself—but that if I purchased the yarn, she'd give me the pattern. I told her I needed needles, too.

I scrutinized the pattern, a photocopy of a hand-drawn chart, as she rang up my purchase. It looked like a mysterious code, a series of lines, dashes, circles, and pyramids drawn on ruled notebook paper. I had no idea what it meant, and it must have shown, because it was at this point that the shop owner asked if I knew how to knit. I bluffed. In my early childhood my grandmother had owned a yarn shop; I spent many hours playing at organizing the buttons and making pom-poms. I'd spent so much of my life surrounded by people who knit, I figured maybe I had learned something through osmosis.

Outside on the street with my prize, it finally sank in: I really didn't know how to knit. Not a clue how to begin. My grandmother had once, for an afternoon, tried to teach me when I was nine or ten. I remember sitting next to her on the couch with long skinny gray needles and some pale-blue acrylic. I remember that the needles were size 4 and that I hated the yarn color. The afternoon ended in frustration with a wonky parallelogram full of holes.

That was the last time I'd held a knitting needle. I was too embarrassed to go back and admit I didn't even know the first stitch, so I beelined to the library for books. I borrowed all the knitting guides I could carry and took them home to decode the pattern. I will never know exactly what it was that I was doing, with those first attempts at forming knits, purls, yarn overs, and knit 2 togethers. But the thing I was making looked nothing like the scarf I'd seen in the window. It was wider, for one thing, and denser despite the size 11 needles. I had to go back to the shop twice for more yarn because I kept running out, and I still wouldn't admit I wasn't sure what I was doing. My finished scarf looked more like a doormat than a lacy lavender cloud. I could not have been more proud of it.

Over the holiday break I went hunting for my next project. I went with my mother to the only yarn shop we could find within an hour's drive of our house. Alma's Yarn was basically two rooms located in the back of the lady's house. She had her yarn arranged in cubbies along the walls. In the center of the room, a table sagged under file boxes filled with pattern leaflets from the sixties and seventies. I selected a collection of scarf patterns modeled by Partridge Family lookalikes because the recommended needle size matched the size 11 needles I already owned. I let my mom show me how to use a cable needle to work a 2-over-2 cable cross, and my next scarf came out very much like it was supposed to. It had fabulous oversize tassels on it. I gave it to my boyfriend, and a week later we broke up. That gave me more time to knit.

Back then, the knitting section at bookstores had slim pickings. Pattern books didn't look like the kinds of clothes I wore. At the library, the knitting collection was primarily from the seventies and eighties, but occasionally I found charming vintage patterns from the forties and fifties. I would photocopy these patterns for lace dresses and Aran pullovers and glue them into sketchbooks. I found a stitch dictionary, and with the reference books I'd found at the library, I started making swatches. I'd knit a few rows, make a mistake and rip it out, then start again. I would rip and reknit the same swatch over and over again. I found a copy of *Knitting Counterpanes* by Mary Walker Phillips and taught myself how to use double-pointed needles to make lacy squares and circles using random bits of worsted or whatever I'd laid my hands on. My yarn stash grew slowly. It consisted mostly of bits of this and that, wool scavenged from rummage sales, my mother's yarn basket leftovers from the seventies that I'd knit and unraveled many times over—a tangled riot of colors and textures that fit into a shoebox.

I moved. In the new city I had few friends and a lot of time to knit.

I worked in a dress shop with another woman who knit. Peggy was in her sixties and had been knitting since she was a teenager. She was a sweater knitter and had fabulous style. She brought me bags of her leftover partial balls of yarn for my swatches and loaned me a copy of *Knitting in America* by Melanie Falick. Even then, I had this vague idea that *Knitting in America* was a seminal work (which it is), and I devoured every word. Next I found Rowan, *Interweave Knits*, and Debbie Bliss. I started sketching croquis and saving my swatches, but I still didn't know how to sew a seam. I tried gloves and mittens but only ever made one from each pair. I still painted, but only in binges for a week or two here and there, less and less often.

There were two yarn shops in nearby towns, but I didn't own a car, so getting to them was difficult. I found that they weren't especially welcoming, so it didn't seem like a great loss. I wasn't involved with any of the local knitting community, either. The online world of knitting was taking off, I was reading all of the knitting blogs, but I didn't know how to insert myself into that conversation. My mom shared my mania for fiber arts, but no one in my social circles did. Mom and I went to the little fiber festivals, the Vermont and New Hampshire sheep and wool festivals that bookend the summer in May and October. The festivals were so full of joy and enthusiasm. The artisans and farmers were passionate about creating beautiful work and anxious to share, not just the work but the skills, too. I felt as if I'd found the bridge I'd been looking for between art and craft.

I learned to spin. Buying prepared fiber by the pound was significantly cheaper than yarn, and the wool was nicer. I dreamed about owning sheep and started methodically spinning sample varieties of wool and other fibers. I started dyeing fiber with Kool-Aid in my kitchen and came home from a sheep and wool festival with an angora rabbit. He roamed freely in my one-bedroom apartment, nibbling the spines off my books and severing my circular needles. He slept at the foot of my bed at night. I called it my urban homestead, before that was a thing. I was finally knitting sweaters, mostly seamless because sewing the knits was still problematic. I improvised a system loosely based on the Elizabeth Zimmermann percentage system. I ripped out as much as I knit.

A friend of the family gave me a Singer home knitting machine from the 1960s. It was a simple bulky machine, which translated to worsted-weight in handknitting yarn. Inspired by the Shetland and Bohus sweaters with their colorwork yokes and machine-knit bodies, I taught myself to use the knitting machine. The increased speed meant that I could produce all the pieces of a sweater in a weekend. The expedited process gave me the momentum to take on set-in sleeve shaping, and I finally learned how to seam knits. As I attempted to keep up with production, the stash exploded. In just a few years it went from a shoebox to a few baskets, then to a yarn closet.

I fell in love and got married. The rabbit was not impressed. We moved to a new town and had a baby. We agreed that I would stay home for the baby's first year, so I left my job. We talked about chickens and sheep and found a little house on a mountain with a couple of acres of land and moved again. Our town had a general store, a post office, and a one-room library that was open four hours a day, four days a week. In rural Vermont you had a waiting list to get DSL Internet access at your house. I drove to the library and sat in the parking lot with my laptop for Wi-Fi while the baby napped. We gardened and raised chickens. We were broke and in love, and it was one of the happiest years of my life. I didn't want go back to work, but I had to earn money. For years, I'd been sketching and swatching ideas for designing knitwear. I'd never written a pattern, but I'd been studying patterns and how they were written. I gave myself an ultimatum: I had to make a profit designing or I would go back to school and get serious about a career. I had one year to make it happen.

Thomas Jefferson wrote, "I am a great believer in luck, and I find the harder I work the more I have of it." For the next year I worked very hard and I was very lucky. I submitted my work to magazines: *Knitty*, *Twist Collective*, and *Interweave Knits*. *Knitty* rejected my submission, but *Knits* accepted my proposal for a raglan jacket with trompe l'oeil lapels worked in intarsia. I had never attempted knit intarsia. It had not occurred to me that the submission might be accepted.

The submission to *Twist Collective* was rejected but came with an encouraging note from Kate Gilbert, the editor. She liked my sketch and the idea, but because I had no portfolio of work to show what I could do, she was going to pass. She encouraged me to try self-publishing to build my résumé and try again. I hadn't really considered this option, since I wasn't online very much—I was still waiting until nap times to go check email in the library parking lot. Ravelry made figuring out self-publishing a lot easier. As I struggled through the intarsia sweater I worked out my scheme: The design fee for the *Interweave* sample would pay for the DSLR camera I'd need to photograph for self-publishing.

The self-publishing exceeded all expectations. People actually bought the patterns. Still checking email from the library once every day or two, it was a shock when I'd sold one copy of a pattern. Then three, then four, and then more. Nine months in, we finally had the Internet coming to our house, and I fumbled my way into learning to engage in social media. About a year into designing I wasn't quite equaling the salary I'd given up when I went on maternity leave, but I was taking in something, enough that it made sense to keep going. I got better at making connections with people online and kept working, making new goals. The more I worked, the more people I met, the more I learned, the more I worked. In the design community, I found a connection with a group of talented, hardworking women, artisans who were anxious to share and learn and support one another. One project led to another that led to another, and suddenly I was very busy.

Saying "Yes" whenever possible, my design business grew. I designed a collection for an Interweave Press book, which flowed into being offered the position of design director at Berroco Yarns. Working in a creative team is a sea change from a life as an independent designer. With the benefit of the four other members of the Berroco design team, we are able to produce exponentially more work than I ever could have before. We design collections, work to produce and publish the patterns, organize photoshoots, and carry out the daily tasks of managing the company's website, marketing, and social media. The yarn industry has two seasons per year. As one collection launches, the design phase of the next has already begun. It is an unrelenting cycle, but the work is a collaboration, and many hands make light work.

There isn't a day when I don't touch yarn. I make with yarn or work with something I made with yarn. It is the path to a creative life, and it sustains me. The stash is limitless. Yarn is everywhere that I am. I go to work in an office warehouse filled with aisles and aisles of yarn, and then I still curl up with a project and knit to unwind at the end of each day. Designing for a living is not unlike the challenges I faced in art school. Create something, then another something, then another. Don't stop. Believing that it should always be done better next time is a powerful motivator. Put the work out there and critique it by sorting out which projects do well or not. The process sometimes feels like finding your way in the dark.

In the Greek myth about the Minotaur, the hero, Theseus, is given a ball of string before he enters the labyrinth to slay the monster. He ties the string to the entrance and lets it unwind as he goes deeper into the dark. Then he follows the string to navigate back out of the Minotaur's maze.

I have found a ball of yarn, and I have been following it through the maze ever since. Each project, book, and the position with Berroco forms a series of sharp angles and turns through the maze. The yarn is my lifeline. I believe that if I keep my hands on yarn, it will guide me through the next series of sharp turns, too.

WHEN IT'S GONE, IT'S GONE
BY CLARA PARKES

Years ago, Roz Chast drew a cartoon about the life cycle of a handknit sweater. I forget the specifics, but it began with a less-than-flattering sweater being gifted by an Aunt Clara at Christmas, which ultimately ended up in a landfill over which grass grew and sheep grazed, starting the cycle all over again. That concept has helped form my personal philosophy of stashing.

I didn't know about the word *stash* for decades. As a lone, occasional knitter growing up in 1980s Tucson, Arizona, and then an equally lone, occasional knitter in San Francisco, I had zero awareness of what other knitters were doing. Once I *did* learn the term *stash*, I had no idea that it was used in any context other than yarn. My exposure to contraband and rule-breaking consisted primarily of a Rowenta toaster I kept in my dorm room throughout college (strictly forbidden). I invited friends over and we had toast parties. BYOJ (bring your own jam).

But I've always had a complicated relationship with "things." This has threatened my relationship to what stash *can* be, versus what I know it *should* be.

My father's side of the family seems quite well-rounded when it comes to letting go of possessions. But my mother's family is a different story that can be summed up as follows: My maternal grandma was famous for the saying, "When it's gone, it's gone." She used it often.

"Would the kids like some gingersnaps?" she'd ask.

"Yes!" we'd cheer.

"Just remember," she'd say as she handed us the plate, "when they're gone, they're gone."

She wasn't being Zen about it; she wasn't urging us to live in the moment and celebrate what we had in the here and now. She spoke like a specter from a Dickens story, the Ghost of Cookies Past, issuing a warning of the profound deprivation and regret that awaited us if we dared use something up. When it's gone, it's gone.

After both my grandparents died, we discovered a freezer in the garage. They'd been out of that house for five years and living in a continuing care community down the road, but the freezer was still plugged in and humming. Inside, we found a fifty-year-old tin of fruitcake, ancient bags of fiddlehead ferns, and trays of perfectly preserved Swedish meatballs from when my mom was in college. Rumor had it a piece of my parents' wedding cake lurked somewhere near the bottom—and they'd been divorced for almost twenty years.

That house, and their apartment down the road, were both packed full. Not with junk, and not to the point of being a public health hazard. They were crammed full of supplies, like a boat packed for a long journey, with extra toys and provisions tucked in every nook and cranny. There were books and records and photographs galore. There were plastic cups from long-ago flights on defunct airlines, all stacked neatly on the kitchen shelf with a note: "Careful not to give to people who crunch cups." There was a full case of Rose's lime marmalade in the dishwasher, it having been on sale and my grandfather being a frugal New Englander (who loved marmalade). There were drawers of my grandma's sewing patterns, all cut out and used and then carefully refolded and repackaged in their envelopes for future reuse. Everything was stored and filed: every single letter they'd received, every bill paid.

After we began dismantling their little house we discovered—or rather, remembered—the two sheds in the yard. They were substantial, nearly as big as the studio I was renting in San Francisco at the time, and they'd been locked up for decades. Each was filled, floor to ceiling, with boxes of yet more things, mostly books; boxes they had never, ever opened; boxes they'd carried out of my grandfather's parents' house in 1970 when *it* was being dismantled. And *that* house? It had been filled with the possessions from *their* parents and grandparents. This holding on to things went back far too many generations to blame the Great Depression, though that definitely did inform my grandma's personal feelings about the finality of things being gone once they're gone. It seemed to be part of a bigger problem: Nobody could get rid of anything.

My parents became a shocking exception. After the divorce, they had a huge garage sale and sold off everything but the bare essentials my mother, brothers, and I needed for our move to Arizona. I think they were both happy to let go of all that old baggage and start fresh. But we were kids, we were scared and lonely, and so we clung. For the first full year we were in Tucson, my brother wore the door key to our old house on a piece of string around his neck.

That move just reinforced my brothers' and my understanding of how "gone" something is after it's gone.

As adults, the three of us were tasked with emptying a total of five homes, two sheds, one barn, one Colonial malt house, and a storage unit. It has been an epic lesson in why you should get rid of stuff, and yet we still can't let go.

Whenever something of sentimental value breaks, my partner, Clare, likes to say, "I'll buy you a new one." She honestly believes anything can be replaced, and she also says it to provoke a very specific response in me. Without a beat, she knows I'll launch into a panicked lament about how that old lightbulb or pair of socks or cracked plastic planter can never, *ever* be replaced. It's *gone*, and as we know, once it's gone . . . it's gone. Eventually I hear myself and realize I've slipped into my old pattern, and I try to let it go.

Then there's yarn.

I used to have a normal, enthusiastic-bordering-on-the-excessive stash, like most knitters. Then I began reviewing yarn professionally. Every week over the course of sixteen years, I would receive boxes and pouches and bags of yarn from manufacturers hoping for coverage, along with skeins I had purchased from other small providers. My stash quickly became two stashes: yarns for my private knitting, and yarns to be reviewed.

One fed the other. I'd discover a new yarn, test it out, fall in love with it, and write its story in *Knitter's Review*. (Which happened more or less on a weekly basis.) I'd panic that once the review came out, the yarn would be gone, and so I'd purchase more, sometimes a sweater's worth, as protection.

My "work" stash was more complicated. Everything came in single skeins, and how many fingerless mitts does one person really need? Not that I would've used those skeins for pleasure, because they'd been intended for work. The bad karma from stealing from that stash would make those mitts rise up and strangle me in my sleep.

By year four of *Knitter's Review*, things were seriously out of control. Luckily (or perhaps because of this), a tradition of a "stash lounge" began at the annual Knitter's Review Retreat I hosted every November. It started as a table, then became several tables, and eventually occupied a whole room.

People deposited yarn they no longer loved or needed or could reasonably use in their lifetime. It was a good crowd, and you knew your yarn would be appreciated. This made it so much easier to let go of the really nice stuff, along with all those impulse purchases, unflattering colors, and skeins with bad memories.

I'd bring giant bags of yarn from both of my stashes, the countless single skeins and a multitude of sweater quantities that never found their way into a sweater. Skeins that carried the heavy baggage of unfulfilled hopes and dreams miraculously shape-shifted into something fresh and inspiring when they entered the stash lounge. It was like a giant karmic washing machine.

Some "work" yarns I've kept even though they were never reviewed and have since been discontinued. Part of my review stash serves as

*Every knitter will be able to pick up a skein
from her stash—any skein—and tell you a
complete and compelling story about it.*

a physical archive of significant moments and trends over the past
sixteen years. Unfortunately for my storage space, there have been
many moments and trends. Every few years I'll sweep through the
archives and deaccession any skeins whose historical significance didn't
end up being all that significant. Because if I kept it all, I'd soon need
another place to live.

Yarn holds energy (literally, twist), but it also holds energy in the
form of memories—like the skeins of Luisa Gelenter's yarn that remind
me of the time I spent with her, or the little blue ball of fingering-weight
I found in my grandma's sewing basket. Every knitter will be able to
pick up a skein from her stash—any skein—and tell you a complete
and compelling story about it.

But there's a very important way in which skeins of yarn differ
from that old house key my brother carried around his neck. Yarn isn't
just an object that holds memories of the past. It is, at its very core,
a tool waiting to be used—all the parts for a sweater, some assembly
required. Comedian George Carlin liked to describe a house as "a pile
of stuff with a cover on it," but a yarn stash is a pile of stuff waiting to
be turned into something beautiful. I have to remind myself of this
distinction every time my yarn starts to pile up.

Some feel best with as little stuff as possible. It makes them feel
nimble, unencumbered. Clare is like that. She'd be fine if we only had
one jar of jam in the house at any given time. (She corrects me: Two
would be better, but three is excessive.) We joke that her ideal furniture
is anything that can be collapsed and tossed into the back of a small car.

I am the opposite. I need the feeling of things around me. I like to have options. I have extra notebooks and fountain pen ink, I have "thank-you" cards for thank-worthy things that haven't yet happened in my life, sympathy cards for yet un-felt losses, birthday cards for birthdays yet to come. I certainly need more than one jar of jam, and I'm fine with furniture that requires two strong men to carry out to a waiting truck. And I absolutely need more than one skein of yarn, or set of needles, or pattern book, or stitch dictionary, to get my creativity going. I like my stash to have a nice big deep end for diving.

But that deep end gets me in trouble. Like stock prices and hemlines, my stash fluctuates. I go through periods when I have total mastery over my stash, when I know exactly what's there and I feel good about it. I'll even feel a little smug. But then I fall into acquisitive phases, times when my soul becomes far hungrier than my consumption merits. I let down my guard for just a minute and my deep end bottoms out.

What was a source of comfort and solace, a collection of things I treasured, has become a barn full of stuff I can no longer see. You should be able to look at your stash and feel inspired to create. But if you can't find anything among heaps of stuff, if you can't *see* your yarn, your stash has stopped working. It no longer inspires creativity.

The irony is that I've written articles about stashbusting, and I even created a Craftsy class about it. I've encouraged people to go

You should be able to look at your stash and feel inspired to create. But if you can't find anything among heaps of stuff, if you can't see your yarn, your stash has stopped working. It no longer inspires creativity.

through their stashes on a regular basis and cull everything that does not bring them joy. I've praised that marvelous feeling you get when you love every skein in your possession. I'm a preacher who constantly grapples with her own faith, the psychotherapist who chose her field to try and heal herself. (The fact that I'm sitting here now, writing about stash for an anthology of my own making, just underlines how complicated the struggle is.)

My knowledge of Buddhism extends primarily to the Dalai Lama's Twitter feed, but I do know that it's not good to cling to material possessions. We are of the nature to die, everything around us is of the nature to die, and there's not a damn thing we can do about it. No amount of yarn or books or old house keys will stop this. All we have is the here and now, and we must live richly in it. I'm not suggesting we renounce possessions, but Buddhist monk Shunryū Suzuki does give a refreshing definition: "Renunciation is not giving up the things of the world, but accepting that they go away."

The universe has a built-in mechanism to help things go away. It's called *entropy*, and it's constantly at work shifting our world from order to disarray, harmony to chaos. Entropy and time can force a tipping point with everything—with clothes or shoes or books or music or yarn, or even with alcohol, food, or cats. There's a tipping point of excess. You know when you've hit it.

Left to its own devices, yarn longs to be in motion. I've witnessed this while making Clara Yarn. I do it the slow way, building relationships with farmers, waiting months until shearing day, then waiting patiently for the fleeces to be skirted, then scoured, then sorted, then carded, spun, twisted, and skeined. Some yarns have been in motion for years before they're ready. Then, I unveil them to the public, and within minutes they are gone. At first, I felt that old panic, the old devastation. These skeins had been my companions for so long and just like that, they were gone. And as we know, when they're gone . . .

But they weren't.

As I watched, the skeins took on a life of their own. Soon they showed up in people's Ravelry stashes and blogs and Instagram feeds and on their bodies as knitted garments. Some hopped from stash to stash, publicly traded on the open market like crude oil or hog futures.

If these skeins continue on their ultimate trajectory, in the distant future the garment will have been worn by as many people as could possibly wear it. The sweater will find its way into the garbage, or a compost pile, or a landfill. It's hard for a knitter to hear, but this step is essential for what happens next. We need that compost and that landfill so that we can grow more grass for the sheep to graze on so that they can—drum roll, please—grow wool for Aunt Clara's next Christmas sweater.

Perhaps there is no beginning and end to yarn, just a constant heartbeat of energy, a long chain of shifting shapes, from lamb to landfill, that started with the Big Bang and won't end until the next Big Bang. All we have, bringing back my inner Buddhist for just a moment, is the here and now. The yarn in our hands and on our needles at this very moment: That's our stash.

SPINNING STASH
BY JILLIAN MORENO

I am a spinner, and my stash is monumental. I will never spin all of it, and I don't care. My stash means far more to me than just yarn to be spun; it makes me a more creative person and a better spinner.

The act of stashing is a creative pursuit all its own. Ask any process crafter. Process crafters don't care if we finish; it's about the planning and the making. Between you and me, I almost never finish anything—maybe one or two projects a year. But that never stops me from planning and starting something new with the same manic glee that my dog greets me with after a few days apart.

Just because I'm a spinner, don't think for one instant that I don't buy yarn or have a commercial yarn stash, too. In fact, I still have yarn bought on my honeymoon in Ireland twenty years ago. It was before the big knitting boom of the late nineties made its way to the United Kingdom, and my husband and I hunted tweed yarn all over the country. We asked about yarn everywhere we saw wool, and we chased down every lead. Finally we found the Donegal Tweed mill, and it was as magical as I wanted it to be, which almost never happens. I got an impromptu tour and was invited to shop mill ends for $1 a skein. We then had to hunt for a duffel big enough to get all the yarn home. We found it: army surplus and huge. This story illustrates not only that I know about the importance of knitting stash, but also why I am still married to my husband after twenty years.

I knit for years, even though I also knew how to spin. And then one day I woke up and needed to spin again. It was soon after number two was born; I was still in that new-baby haze, just trying to shower every day and have enough wits about me to play with number one

A spinning stash is much more complex than a knitting stash. It is like the first mother goddess. Everything comes from it, and nothing happens without it. You can't have yarn without the fiber.

when she came home from school. I'd known how to spin for eight or so years by then, though I had put it aside. But I woke up that day with a fierce need to spin and to make yarn. I got out my wheel, which had been waiting patiently, made some seriously ugly yarn, and haven't looked back.

Spinning was all the things I loved about knitting but with so many more options and decisions, so many more yarns to make and then use or admire. My spinning stash grew faster than my knitting stash ever did. It was like fireflies in the summer—you see one, turn and call "there are fireflies!" into the house, then look again and they are everywhere.

A spinning stash is much more complex than a knitting stash. It is like the first mother goddess. Everything comes from it, and nothing happens without it. You can't have yarn without the fiber.

When I make my own yarn, I get to choose the fiber—the breed of sheep, the type of silk, the flax, cotton, steel, or blend. I select or create the preparation, whether it's commercial top or roving, batts, fleeces to be washed and combed or carded, or locks to spin in. I decide on the size of my yarn, the drafting technique, the number of plies—all to make the exact yarn I want for a project or an idea in my head.

Then there's color. Color in the spinning stash isn't just about what you buy. There are natural and dyed solids, semisolids, variegateds, and gradients that can be manipulated and combined in spinning in an infinite number of ways to create an equally infinite number of color effects.

Each of these choices informs my finished yarn, and my stash reflects all of this boundless possibility. I have fleeces, top, roving, batts (smooth and wild), rolags, punis, several kinds of silk, and a raft of dyed fiber. That's my favorite part of my stash. That corner looks like the sky on the fourth of July—an explosion of color, and a celebration of the talented dyers from whom I've bought my fiber.

As a spinner, this thinking and decision-making happens before I ever knit one stitch. It's what keeps me excited about spinning and keeps me adding to my stash.

I could never have too much fiber. I never felt the same way about commercially spun knitting yarn. In fact, I was happy to de-stash those skeins, giving them away to knitters who wanted them. My knitting stash was about acquisition; my spinning stash touches something deeper.

Looking back, I realize I have always had stashes. I grew up in a not-so-friendly family during the 1970s, when no one used words like *dysfunction*, and no matter how haunted you looked, no one outside of your family could do much to help you. While my parents focused on their own sorrows and misery, I gathered things. For me it was books and stuffed animals. The books let me know there were other places and people—a path out. The animals gave me something tactile to hang on to, literally.

As I was growing up, I believed in myself and made a few important, not always easy choices. I walked away from the people who hurt me or didn't support me, including my parents and lots of so-called friends. Then I walked—no, I ran—toward people who loved and supported me in my life, my work, my play.

Those choices allowed me to find joy and satisfaction in whatever calls me. I no longer gather things as a shield from the grief of my childhood. I still have a hefty number of books, and they still show me places and people, but now they are a celebration of humanity. The stuffed animals have been replaced with fiber, every ounce of which symbolizes potential—the potential to become yarn, and the potential to fuel my own creativity.

I am a magpie, a collector. If I am interested in something, I want it, *all of it*. Tweed yarn? I want a skein of every kind I can find and all the books about it, too. I use stash for research. I stockpile against trauma and tragedy and to feed my curiosity. I am not a completist. Loads of fiber, for stash's sake, nothing more, make me happy.

A lot of my stashing has to do with what-ifs. What if I:

- Get snowed in
- Want to start something in the middle of the night
- Lose my job or have no money to spend on stash
- Find it on sale
- Get a discount
- Find my favorite color
- Find my favorite fiber
- Encounter a wool shortage
- Fear someone else might buy it
- Realize that someone I know needs it, in a
  snowstorm, in the middle of the night . . .

You get the idea, and probably have some similar anxieties.

A spinner needs a stash that reflects the monumental potential in yarn. Add to this the what-ifs, the wild hairs, and the abject failures, and the need for stash just keeps growing.

I am unapologetic about the size of my stash. It keeps me grounded. In it I see possibility and the comfort of abundance. It is a reflection of me on a deep level. It's also filled with connections. Not just the stories of what happened and who I was with when I bought a particular braid of fiber, but also the stories of the fiber and where it came from. The closer you get to the source, the closer you get to the people.

Buy a braid of fiber produced by a commercial yarn manufacturer at your local yarn store, and you'll meet all of the wonderful people at your shop. Buy a hand-dyed braid from the dyer herself at a fiber fair, and you'll meet the person who dyed it and possibly even sourced and processed it. Buy a fleece from a shepherd, and you'll meet the sheep (whose name is Lavender), learn about the flock and shepherd, and possibly sit down and have coffee and cookies with her and end up going back every year after shearing to pick up more fleeces. All of those stories and communities orbit around my stash.

But what's most important to me about my stash is that it makes me more creative.

A big stash allows me to have a fluid sense of creativity—a looseness that is very much like playing. It opens me up, unlocks things. The creative bit takes all the other pieces—the possibility, the abundance, the connections, and the actual work of making yarn—bundles them, and explodes like a glitter bomb. It gets everywhere, it makes me smile, and I can't escape it.

My stash is the spark. Even if I haven't spun for days or weeks, even when I'm feeling dull-witted or anti-craft, I still spend time with my stash. It pulls on doors that have been locked, slides under the crack and clicks them open from the inside. After an hour tossing my fibers around, I am revitalized for making yarn, yes, but for things well beyond that, too. My stash feels like an extension of me that I sometimes forget about: the part that plays, that connects things that don't seem to go, that experiments and makes things.

Over the years, I've discovered some spinners who are actually intimidated by their stash. They're ashamed of it, confused or overwhelmed by it, stuck in ruts because of it, or just not really spinning happily from it. I want to pass along the feeling my stash brings me. Whenever I teach, I bring a duffel bag of fibers culled from my own stash, and I offer it up like bread starter.

I dump its contents in the middle of the floor. The room goes silent. There is an instant tension, as when a terrier sees a squirrel. The students have laser focus. There is burbling excitement. They don't know what's going to happen, but it's going to be good, because there is stash.

We start with one or two fibers. I ask them to pick. They are always kind, never snatching, but they are focused. They grab what speaks to them. Some do exactly what I ask of them, some need a little extra. There are always a few people who will boldly take more than their share—some sneak it and hide it in their bag. I understand that need. Somewhere in their life they didn't get enough. Let this be the time that they do.

Then there are those who gaze at the pile. They take just enough, maybe a little less. But they keep staring, and I know they need more. They're holding themselves back. They don't play enough, they don't give enough to themselves. Sometimes I give them extra, and when I do, their whole self smiles and I hear, faintly, a sort of *click*. Something has unlocked.

It is a visceral and amazing process. As we work, my students keep diving into the stash. I see them change; they are free and joyous. Concepts they found harder to get or didn't think they'd like come easier. There is lightness. They are digging in and instinctively playing—spinning differently. I know that they won't look at their own stash the same way when they get home.

Since that fateful morning so many years ago, my number two has grown and is now in middle school, and number one is on her way to college. And my spinning stash? It's become big and messy like Jo Anne Worley's uncontrolled laugh, spilling everywhere and bringing lightness and play into my life—and that's exactly how I want it.

STASH-CHANGING MOMENTS
BY SUSAN B. ANDERSON

I taught myself to knit as a teenager. Knitters weren't in my family or even in my neighborhood, for all I knew, so I learned on my own. There was no Internet, and there really weren't any knitting books at the bookstore. It was a different time.

I immediately fell in love with knitting, though, and I set out to learn everything I could about yarn, tools, and techniques. What I didn't know anything about, however, was stashing or collecting yarns. I would simply find a pattern, buy the yarn for that pattern, and then knit that pattern with that yarn. It was the only way I knew.

After I had been knitting for several years, I learned that my friend's mom, who happened to own a yarn shop in a quaint little city a couple of hours' drive from where I lived, was looking to retire and sell her shop. When she told me, my heart stopped for a minute. I wondered if this was supposed to be the next chapter in my life.

The yarn shop was in a historic mill, which made it even more charming and enticing. The old stone walls, the nearby wooden walking bridge, the flowers, the creek that trickled by the back side of the shop, the huge rooms inside, and the shelves already chock-full of colorful, squishy yarns—the whole scenario was pretty much a dream. I talked to my friend's mom and asked if she would consider me taking over the shop for her, and she said yes! It was all very preliminary, as I had small children at home and a husband with a good job he liked, and we lived in another city. But I loved thinking about the potential of that knit shop.

I arranged to visit the store just to spend a day and hang out. While there, I learned a thing or two about knitting that would change my life forever. I walked in that morning and was greeted by an attractive, tall, and friendly woman named Ann. Ann was knitting away as she introduced herself, working on a gray sweater of some sort with the ball of yarn tucked under her arm. I was fascinated right off the bat. She had worked at the shop for years. She made me feel comfortable, and we began to chat about knitting, as knitters do. I didn't even know any knitters at the time, and I basically had never talked to anyone about knitting. I was starved for information and ready to get my fill of knitting talk with Ann.

She asked me about my knitting. I pulled out a baby hat I was working on. I was at the decrease point on the crown, where it was getting too small to fit comfortably around my sixteen-inch circular needle. I had double-pointed needles with me, but I had no idea how to use them. I shyly asked Ann, who quickly showed me how the needles worked. Within a second I was on my way. I was overjoyed.

I asked her how she found time to knit during her busy days. She woke up at 5:00 every morning, before her family got out of bed. She made a cup of coffee and would sit and knit for a couple of hours in total peace and quiet. I had honestly never thought about doing that. It was an incredible idea, similar to athletes training early in the morn-ing. Being an early bird by nature, I took this idea to heart and have been spending the wee hours of the morning knitting in peace with a cup of hot coffee by my side ever since.

The final topic that came up in our conversation was stash. I had never heard or thought of collecting yarn before. Ann told me about her stash of yarns, some lined up for specific projects but most without purpose as of yet. It was this second type of stash that was new to me. She told me that she would buy yarns from different shops, yarn that was made in different cities or countries, and yarns that she ran across in her travels—without any project in mind. I was completely naïve about the concept of stash, but I fell in love with it. I left the shop that day with my head spinning about yarn and knitting and a whole new knitting lifestyle that I really wanted to dive into fully.

We ended up not buying the quaint yarn shop by the creek. My husband got another job offer that was closer to home, and we happily moved on. However, my knitting was never the same after that visit; it became so much more. I started thinking about yarn and stash in a completely different way. I slowly started looking at yarns and their potential to become all sorts of things, not just one specific project. Thinking about stashing yarns like this expanded my intentions and my ideas about projects. Ideas swirled in my mind about designing with different yarns. It was a whole new world.

I started to collect my own stash.

Years have gone by since that brief yarn-shop fantasy. My knitting life, and stash, have changed. I am now a full-time knitting author, writer, and designer. My life's work, besides raising my family, has become all about knitting, yarn, and that once missing stash. I have traveled to teach at yarn festivals, yarn markets, and yarn shops all over the country and beyond. While at these events I often explore the cities and event markets and buy special yarn souvenirs to take home with me to remind me of that place and time. Needless to say, my stash has grown. I also have boxes and boxes of yarn show up on my doorstep from yarn companies either to design with or to review. This is a pretty fun problem to have, and I'm not complaining. But over time, my stash got a bit out of hand. Every nook, cubby, bin, and drawer in my little house had been taken over by stash.

Then something happened. I heard the fantastic knitwear designer Hannah Fettig discussing her stash on a podcast, and it struck a resounding chord with me. Hannah said she realized that her growing stash was stressing her out. She wasn't enjoying it any longer. Instead of dwelling on it, she packed it all up and took it to her local knit night. Hannah made a bold move and simply gave her entire stash away, saving only the few yarns she needed for current design projects. She described how an enormous weight of guilt and burden was lifted off her shoulders. Hannah's actions had a big impact on me. I, too, was feeling stress about my yarn stash, and something needed to be done about it.

I wanted to shed my stash like a snake shedding its old skin. After being completely inspired by Hannah's brave act, I decided to try something similar. It seemed unavoidable. I started looking at my yarn collection in a new light, studying the skeins and thinking about what the different yarns meant to me. I devised a plan to sort my stash into four simple categories.

Category 1: My desire to work with this yarn has changed. It has to go.

Category 2: This yarn is for current works in progress. It has to stay.

Category 3: These are special memory skeins from travels, gifts, or even virtual travel (I snagged a special skein online that I'd been eyeing forever from a British farm, for example). These yarns can either be saved or let go, but an immediate decision has to be made.

Category 4: This yarn is appropriate for giveaways on my blog or for workshops. It stays. This isn't a universal need for most knitters, so I will leave it mostly out of this conversation.

Caveat: One yarn type that I fudged a little was sock yarn. I am a sock knitter who tears through her sock yarn stash quickly, so I put these skeins into the work-in-progress category even if the sock wasn't currently on my needles. I think that's fair.

I started going through my stash one drawer, one cubby, one bin at a time. Every skein in my stash was touched and considered and then immediately placed in a sorting category. It took days to get through it all, and at times it was a bit painful to make hard decisions. When I finished sorting that final bin of yarn, I felt a total calm. I never changed

Every skein in my stash was touched and considered and then immediately placed in a sorting category. It took days to get through it all, and at times it was a bit painful to make hard decisions. When I finished sorting that final bin of yarn, I felt a total calm.

my mind or regretted any decision I had made. I'd made huge progress.

I ended up with an enormous pile of Category 1 yarns, the part of my stash that had to go. The smallest pile was Category 2, yarns for current works in progress. It was easy to assign these yarns: either I needed that yarn for a current project, or I didn't. If there were works in progress that had been sitting for a long time, I ripped them out, wound up the yarn, and added it to the "has to go" pile.

Category 3 was the hardest part of the stash to sort through. It was a trip down memory lane to look at the special skeins I had collected through the years; many skeins brought back happy memories, ties to people, and knitting adventures. These yarns all had a purpose and meaning attached at one point in time, but hard decisions had to be made. In the end I saved some of the special skeins I had collected, but not all. For example, a student in one of my classes had given me a skein of her handspun fingering-weight yarn for me to knit socks, and the fiber was from one of my favorite indie dyers. This was a keeper skein for sure. Donegal Yarns had sent me two skeins of Studio Donegal Soft Tweed in the richest shade of pumpkin, all the way from Ireland, to use or review. These skeins will stay in the stash, and I will eventually design something wonderful with this treat of a yarn. Sometimes things have to stay with you.

All the Category 1 yarns went to my neighbor. She does charity knitting through her church, and her group does fantastic work in our community. The yarns that I saved? They're now freshly organized, savored, and truly loved with new purpose. We all need to clean our stashes, especially ones that have grown to be unruly over the years. It frees up both physical and mental space, and that feels good. If you don't have a stash yet or you want to start fresh, my advice is to try to be thoughtful and purposeful with your stash collecting. Most important, don't overdo it. Now whenever I am tempted to purchase yarn, I think of my three sorting categories, and most of the time I walk away. Being able to enjoy your stash will make you a better and happier knitter in the end.

I've learned so much since my visit with Ann at the dreamy little knit shop so many years ago. She will never know the incredible impact those few hours had on me, my knitting, and my stash.

If you don't have a stash yet or you want to start fresh, my advice is to try to be thoughtful and purposeful with your stash collecting. Most important, don't overdo it.

WORK IN PROGRESS
BY LILITH GREEN

I can't remember a time when I wasn't aware of my body, or how it appeared to other people. Anyone who grew up female will probably understand how it feels to be constantly bombarded with a stream of messages about the female body and its value (or lack thereof).

- *Be thin, but not too thin.*
- *Be "curvy," but not fat.*
- *Wear makeup, but not too much.*
- *Look feminine, but not too "girly."*
- *Don't dress in anything dowdy or "unflattering."*
- *Look sexy, but not slutty.*

It's exhausting, and it's everywhere. It's so pervasive that even the smartest women I know (myself included) fall prey to it.

The first time I tried to lose weight, I set up a system of "rewards" that I thought would help me get to my goal weight. With each chunk of weight I lost, I bought myself something fancy—a boutique dress, a pair of high-heeled boots, expensive fitted jeans. The final reward for hitting my target weight was a new tattoo—it's the only thing I still have, after (inevitably) putting most of the weight back on. More than five years later, I've realized what I was doing to myself. My subconscious rationale was that only thin girls deserve nice clothes; that nobody wants to see a fat girl in tight jeans or sexy boots. My "rewards" were actually punishments, designed to shame me into staying thin.

This is how the Western beauty system is set up; this is what years of programming do to you. You're not allowed to choose clothes just because you like them, or wear makeup because it's a fabulous color. If you're unlucky enough to have a body that doesn't conform to the restrictive (and frankly, ridiculous) beauty standards, clothing and makeup aren't things to be enjoyed—they exist only to "help" you. Women's magazines, the diet industry, and fast fashion to the rescue. "Hide your problem areas!" "Disguise your flaws!" Just buy this beauty product, this makeup, this dress, this top. And if those don't work, buy some more stuff, and keep buying stuff, and eventually all your body problems will be solved.

Even when I started knitting and sewing, taking my first steps outside of the world of fast fashion, I still struggled. I did knit beautiful sweaters from gorgeous yarns for my partner, whose body type doesn't change shape too often and whose broad shoulders look fantastic in handknits. And although I managed to knit these to fit perfectly, the few garments I made for myself often ended up unloved and unworn. I had such a distorted view of my body that they were inevitably hugely oversize, or a style I didn't actually like but that I thought would be "suitable" for someone my shape and size. I dyed luxurious yarns of every hue for knitters all over the world, but my personal stash had a lot of muted colors (why call attention to my body with bright, bold shades?) and a high proportion of sock and lace-weight yarns (socks and shawls will still fit, I reasoned, even if my weight changes—even if I'm fat).

Over time and over a few more years of losing and gaining weight, I could sense that my view of my body was gradually shifting. My partner was seriously ill for nearly two years before doctors worked out what was going on (and, thankfully, were able to help). The toll this took made me wonder why I was so worried about how I looked from the outside when I was lucky enough to have everything working properly on the inside. Watching Stephen West's knitting patterns develop and his "more is more, less is a bore" attitude toward color and style; discovering Sonya Philip's "100 Acts of Sewing" and her simply structured but amazingly beautiful fashion sense; starting online yoga classes with Jessamyn Stanley—all of these things combined to help me forge a new attitude toward my body, and a new direction toward making and the materials I used.

When I first started knitting, and later, sewing, I spent hours browsing Ravelry, knitting blogs, and sewing blogs looking for photos of finished garments. Is it okay for me to invest the time and money into making this for myself? Did someone who looks like me knit or sew this already? How does it look on them? Is it flattering? Eventually I realized what I meant by "flattering" was actually, "If I make this, will it make me look thinner? Younger? More conventionally attractive? Will it solve my body problems?"

But here's the thing that I've only just started to figure out: My body is not a problem to be solved.

It has survived years of not enough food, too much caffeine, and too little sleep (otherwise known as "university"). It has gained weight, and lost it, and gained it again. It has acquired scars and tattoos, tan lines and stretch marks, wrinkles and freckles and gray hairs. It has fought off illness and healed itself from injury. It has slogged through a Tough Mudder, run for miles without stopping, walked a marathon. It is an incredible, beautiful machine that does so many things so well. And now, in its fortieth year, I am finally teaching myself not to hate it. Not to love it, either; not yet. But I am a work in progress, and one day I will.

I will do this yard by yard, with folds of fabric and strands of yarn. As I tuck fat skeins of wool in next to their sisters, I plot the thick cabled sweater that will hug my slightly-older-and-stiffer bones through next year's damp, cold winter. Bright, multicolored sock yarns will become simple socks to hug the feet that hold me up each day and bring some cheer to gray mornings. A precious skein of luminously hand-dyed, gloriously soft cashmere will become a luxurious, intricate lace shawl fit for a queen, which will most likely live on the back of my armchair

I stash for the body I have now and will have for years to come. Not for the body others think I should have, or that I think I should have, but this body, here and now. It will always have faults and flaws, weaknesses and whims, but it also has such strength, beauty, and power that it takes my breath away.

to be dragged on over ancient pajamas against a chilly draft (in fact, I should probably sew myself some new pajamas as well).

I fold away the washed linen that will become simple loose-fit trousers, soft against the legs that have carried me safely and sturdily over so many miles. This bolt of strong corduroy will be a work jumpsuit/overalls—completely "unflattering" and a complete joy to wear—that make me feel like Rosie the Riveter. The scraps of a vintage Superman bedsheet (the larger part of which has already been made into a SuperDress of power and confidence) are being hoarded for secret pockets or cuff facings, so I can sew superpowers into everything I make. And the shimmering vintage silk sari is taken out of my stash every few days to be unfolded and refolded, as I imagine the bias-cut slip or slinky dress it might become. There are some parts of my body that I struggle to love more than others, and I'm not ready to start this project yet, but I know it's waiting in my stash when I am.

I stash for the body I have now and will have for years to come. Not for the body others think I should have, or that I think I should have, but this body, here and now. It will always have faults and flaws, weaknesses and whims, but it also has such strength, beauty, and power that it takes my breath away. It will always be mine, and I will enrobe it in as much splendor as I can muster—this is my body of work.

THE COMFORT YARN
BY RACHAEL HERRON

I'm not much of a stash person.

Before you roll your eyes or sigh with disappointment, please know this: I've *been* a stash person. Boy, howdy, have I ever been one.

I've had stash stacked from floor to ceiling. I've tried every single method of stash storage, and I've made some up. I've denied it. I've hidden it. I've thrown out receipts to avoid the shame, and I've done the opposite: I've left them out in the open, along the same lines as sticking an unflattering picture of yourself on the refrigerator.

By nature, I'm a magpie. I'm a collector of pretty things. Given the right nudge, I could slip quite easily into hoarding, and I know that about myself, so I urge myself in the other direction. A few years ago, I read Marie Kondo's book (you know, the one about the magic of tidying up—you either hate it or you love it, there is no in-between when it comes to KonMari). After reading it, I swung to the minimalist side. I looked forward to parting with stash, but I had no idea how much it would exhilarate me. Almost three years later, I haven't missed one single skein. Not one. (That should come as comfort if you *want* to part with some stash but worry about regret.) I don't go window shopping much anymore. I don't cruise Internet yarn stores. I buy what I need to make something when I want to make it, and that feels good.

But you know what? I kept some. I didn't get rid of *all* my stash.

I kept my sock yarn (because you always need to be able to cast on for another pair, immediately), cashmere (because if you need cashmere, you need it instantly), and handspun (because dang it, I don't spin that much and the stuff I do spin I'm awfully and probably unreasonably proud of).

Those are the reasons.

But they're not the whole truth.

The deepest truth behind why I kept a few small boxes of yarn is this: To feel safe, I need to have a stash for comfort knitting. In the same way you buy an extra sympathy card just to have around, I need to have comfort yarn close at hand.

A few months ago, I got a phone call from one of my best friends. I can count on one hand how many times she's actually called me. We send texts. We email. We don't *call* unless it's an emergency. So I answered.

I didn't recognize her voice. It was guttural. Desperate.

"My son." She gave a gasping sound. "Has been killed."

A car accident out on the winding coastal highway had killed her only child, twenty-four-year-old Sergio Klor de Alva.

"On my way." My fingers fumbled with my phone—I couldn't seem to remember how to hang up. The only thing I needed in that moment was to be with Julie. I'm smart enough to know that my presence wouldn't fix a thing, but I wasn't going to breathe again until I was parked in front of her, one arm around her shoulders, the other arm protecting her from any further harm (as if anything could ever hurt her again).

I didn't change out of my yoga clothes. I grabbed my keys and wallet. I was ready to go in seconds, and each one counted.

The only thing I slowed down to get was my knitting.

Nothing I'd been already knitting would do, of course. In a tragedy, I need something new, something I hope can hold—absorb—some of the pain. My ever-present socks wouldn't do—they were too thin, too fiddly. I couldn't work on the sweater I was making for my sister—there was no way I'd be able to concentrate on the armscye decreases.

The softest yarn I had immediately at hand was a skein of blue Merino lace-weight. It wasn't wound into a ball. I grabbed a circular needle. I had no plan, no pattern. It didn't matter.

I ran.

Hours later, while making phone calls to the morgue and the sheriff's department, I unwound the skein. I draped the loop over the back of one of Julie's antique, mismatched wooden chairs. I listened to a nightmarish hold message from the highway patrol that seemed to never end: "Be careful on our highways. One lapse of attention is the difference between life and death. Never drink and drive. Don't be the person to cause that kind of pain to the ones who love you most." The fact that I was making a center-pull ball using my thumb as a nostepinne was the only reason I didn't climb right into the phone line to punch out the recording (for the record, toxicology reports later showed Sergio had been under the influence of nothing but fatigue from the low-paid social activism job he loved).

Winding the yarn allowed my brain a place to rest. Making a perfect center-pull ball was productive, in a way that being on hold for hours wasn't.

That night, at Julie's kitchen table, I cast on. The house was full then, dozens of Julie's closest friends filling the rooms with love and grief.

One person sliced homemade bread. No one was eating, but at least she had a job, something to do. Another person went around refilling wineglasses. Yet another friend monitored Sergio's Facebook page, showing his mother the best pictures, the kindest notes.

I cast on forty stitches.

"What are you making?" Kendall, usually quick with a bawdy joke and a cheeky wink, looked desperate for my answer.

"I don't know."

"Oh." Disappointment flared her cheeks red. "Can I help?"

I wished she could. I wished that Kendall could tell me what in the world I was doing with that yarn, but she couldn't. And I didn't know.

I knit for a while.

That night, at home, I threw the knitting still on its needle into the closet, right into my dirty clothes hamper.

It wasn't right.

It hadn't helped.

The next morning, I chose a ball of chunky gray wool that I'd bought at Stitches West. I'd planned on making a sweater out of the twelve-hundred yards I had of it, but that didn't make sense, not that day. I picked another needle and drove to Julie's house and spent the day making phone calls and trying to decide what to make with the yarn that suddenly felt too stiff, too sturdy, too rough.

It reminded me of the time I'd knit while my mother was dying. I'd had the same problem then. No yarn was right. I finished a sweater (a copy of one she'd gotten in Norway in the sixties) at her bedside, and I was left with empty, desperate hands.

She lived five hours away from my own stash, so I went to the local yarn shop in her town, a store I'd never visited. The women working there reminded me of my friends at home. I didn't tell them why tears were running down my face as I wandered the aisles touching the skeins, but I bet they had a good guess I needed yarn therapy in a bad way. Suddenly unable to face color or cheer of any kind, I bought four skeins of dark black yarn, an alpaca-wool blend that felt as heavy as my soul.

Later, in my mother's room, when people asked what I was making, I said it was a prayer shawl. "How sweet," they said. "She'll love that." I knew, though, that it wasn't for her. It was for me. The things I tucked into each stitch were *my* hopes, *my* unanswered prayers. I knew then I'd never finish the shawl, and indeed I didn't. When Mom died, I didn't even finish the row. I bagged the project. Years later, I gave it away to a craft reuse shop. It didn't feel good to knit it, and how could it have?

Here's the thing. As makers, we fix things. That's what we do. It's our superpower. We're good at it.

When it comes to grief and loss, though, there's no fixing.

Here's the thing. As makers, we fix things. That's what we do. It's our superpower. We're good at it. When it comes to grief and loss, though, there's no fixing.

No wonder our stashes can seem so powerless in those times. There is no magic skein of Cormo that will fix our brother's cancer. There's nothing on two sticks that can ease radiation fatigue.

But our stash isn't for them.

It's for us.

It's how we show up, and there's nothing more important than just that. Being present.

Having the right yarn at hand at the very worst times is how we *get there.*

While we helped Julie plan Sergio's services, the house stayed full. People sat in every room, and so many of them had wide stares, fidgeting hands. Some people cooked. Others dropped cartons of coffee and donut deliveries and ran. Chris did the dishes, by hand. He refused to let even a single glass end up in the dishwasher.

I had my knitting, and I couldn't imagine *not* having it. With it, I could sit still. I could meet every gaze as my fingers kept moving. I could converse. More importantly, I could listen as the stitches moved in my fingers.

Without my knitting, I don't know if I would have been brave enough to stay. I might have run away—helpless—like so many other people who came in and out of the house.

Without anything To Do, people ran.

Knitting, in grief, gives me bravery. It's my armor.

Am I giving you permission to bolster your stash with more yarn? Hell yes, I am. This is the only time I'll advise you to stock up.

Buy it without a plan. Stash it in a box that pleases you. Mark it if you like: COMFORT YARN.

The actual yarn you buy is inconsequential. It can be a seventy-dollar ball of cashmere or that soft two-buck baby yarn from Michael's. The only thing comfort yarn should be is soft and pleasing to both the hand and the eye. Stripes or soft gradients are nice, giving your gaze a place to rest, but they aren't necessary.

Nor do you need a pattern. In fact, I'd argue against one. Connecting the printer and casting on a certain precise number of stitches and getting gauge can be too stressful in these times.

Just cast on using whatever needle you think might work. Knit awhile. Purl if you feel like it. Do a little seed stitch. Change your mind? Pull it out and start over. Do this ten times. Then ten more, if it helps you sit and be present.

As a product knitter, this is the one time I'm only about process. I do not care about the end product, not one little bit. I spent last weekend with my mother-in-law, who's dying slowly of a painful disease that we can't stop or predict. Packing at the last minute, I threw in three fat skeins of yarn I'd spun on my wheel the month before. On the circular needle I'd brought, I cast on one-by-one rib. I knit a short, fat scarf (because that's what it turned into) until I ran out of yarn. On the plane home, I did a half-twist and joined the ends with a three-needle bind-off and ended up with a cowl that will always remind me of the coffee shop where we all sat outside and pretended everything was okay when it really, really wasn't. The fact that it actually turned into something was just a side effect. In the sun next to my mother-in-law, I held my yarn and needles and I was able to just sit.

To be.

To breathe with her.

Makers are doers. We're often not content to just sit with open hands and watch life pass by—we have to get up and accomplish something, anything. Put us in front of a television with nothing in our fingers, and we'll manage six or seven minutes before we're off the couch and searching for something else to do.

At Julie's house, I finally ended up knitting with stashed red cashmere. I knit a square and made it into a long rectangle. I didn't need it to be anything. My knitting couldn't fix her pain. I could do nothing.

In grief and loss, it's often true that there's nothing we can do. We can't fix it. We can't change it. The only thing we *can* do (and by far the very best thing to do) is to show up. Again and again. You arrive and sit and stay. There is only so much puttering and card-moving and flower-arranging that can be done before you sit and look at the person you love, the person in pain.

With soft yarn in your hands and no plan beyond moving this stitch to that needle, it's easy to stay.

So yes, go shopping. Tragedy happens to all of us, and while I hope it's decades before it happens to you, I urge you to fill that box.

And I recommend cashmere.

A PROPER STASH
BY KRISTINE VEJAR

From a very young age, I've had an astute understanding of what constitutes proper dress attire. My grandmother did not wear pants or athletic shoes. A knee-length skort and white Keds were okay to prune the roses. Other than that, it was a uniform of dresses and skirts paired with oxford shirts, made from cotton, preferably with a touch of polyester to help control the dreaded wrinkle. Permissible colors were neutrals, periwinkle, and, every once in a while, a fuchsia-colored blouse, for just a pop of color. The overarching message: Look your best without calling too much individual attention. Belonging was of key importance.

I spent my summers with my grandmother, learning to sew and knit, and I grew to know her circle of friends—many of whom were prolific quilters. Each quilter's home functioned as her own private gallery. The bed, a stand-in for the museum wall, displayed the main work of art. Sitting on a bed topped with a handmade quilt was a crime akin to shoplifting or swiping a couple bucks off the top of the donation basket passed during Sunday mass. Quilts were a combination of performance art, created in a group, and plein-air art, not to be touched, only to be looked at, with the women of the house acting as security guards, protecting the household Van Gogh. These quilts would be passed down to future generations, always with the hope that generations to come would also stitch their own quilts, adding to the collection.

Because my grandmother gave such attention to her choice of dress, since early childhood I have been keen to people-watch with specific attention to the way people wear and style their clothing. It should come as no surprise that, when I traveled to India years later as part of a study-abroad program, I would be drawn to a community of women who also have a very astute idea of what constitutes proper dress attire—and also have an intense custom and history of stitching.

In India, it is common and stylish for Hindu women to wear brightly colored saris. But the Rabari women in the Great Rann of Kutch (a desert region in the northwest corner of India) wear primarily all black, and they do not wear saris. I was drawn to them immediately. Their daily outfit is composed of an ankle-length skirt, a blouse with elbow-length sleeves, and a very large, woolen, rectangular headscarf worn just over the crown of the head, cascading down over their shoulders to just above the back of the knee. Sometimes, bright, colorful embroidery, speckled with tiny mirrors, dances across the front of a blouse.

Seeing the Rabari, words that come to mind are *regal, modern, striking,* and *beautiful severity.* The Rabari's unusual and distinctive style of dress made me curious to know why and how it came to be, and to learn more about their textile traditions. Was this an adaptation to their environment? Did the Rabari stitch together, like my grandmother and her friends? Did they create textiles other than what they wore? Their style of going outside of the norm led me to believe that this type of independent thinking would reflect in their other textiles, too. Over the course of the next two years, I met many Rabari women. I interviewed them about their textiles, and this is what I learned.

Historically, the Rabari spent hours, sometimes days and nights, roaming the desert with their cows and goats, a camel trailing at their side, carrying their belongings and sometimes a child or an elder. When they weren't walking, the women stitched. Rabari women sewed all of their own clothing (along with their children's and most of their husbands'). They embroidered their blouses and headscarves, and they appliquéd larger, utilitarian objects, like bags and quilts.

Embroidery is a popular pastime throughout the Great Rann

Embroidery is a popular pastime throughout the Great Rann of Kutch, where many people find themselves in living conditions similar to those of the Rabari. To embroider and appliqué, only small amounts of materials are needed—a small and portable stash that suits their nomadic lifestyle.

of Kutch, where many people find themselves in living conditions similar to those of the Rabari. To embroider and appliqué, only small amounts of materials are needed—a small and portable stash that suits their nomadic lifestyle. Such materials are lightweight and easy to carry, which is important when covering hundreds of miles on foot through the desert. Where money is saved in the realm of materials, time is spent to create elaborately decorated textiles, especially in the case of the Rabari.

To set themselves apart and recognize one another from far distances while walking in the desert, the Rabari developed their own distinct style. When they embroider, they create flowers, mandalas, and curving, flowing borders to tie it all together. Their appliqué takes a pictorial form depicting elephants, flowers, and peacocks. Motifs, in combination with the specifically chosen color palette and set repertoire of stitches, like the commonly used chain stitch, are what define a quintessential Rabari textile. Just like my grandmother's desire to belong, the same holds true for a Rabari woman. Her textiles form a bond between her and her community.

The day a Rabari woman is married is the most celebrated event in her life. For the wedding, a ceremonial camel blanket would be made. Unique to the Rabari, this piece looks like a rectangle where the four corners have been elongated, with tassels made of scrap fabric attached to each end. A quilt would be made for the bride and groom to sit on. As part of her dowry, the woman would make bags to carry her belongings, including that stash of embroidering materials. If the family she was marrying into lived in a house, she might make wall hangings, too. She also would transition to wearing a special wardrobe of clothing signifying her status as a married woman.

There are three groups of Rabari who are defined by where in the desert they live and by the subtle differences in their embroidery and appliqué. They are the Kaachi, Vaghadia, and Dhebaria. As I traveled around the desert, I began to notice stacks of Dhebaria Rabari textiles and clothing for sale. This was unusual—it was rare to see a Rabari piece for sale, most having been tucked away for safekeeping. These stacks of textiles had the finest, tiniest stitches I had ever seen. And these stitches covered the entire surface of the fabric. The combination of stitch and color made the motifs come alive and nearly dance off the pieces. Of the three communities, the Dhebaria Rabari created the finest textiles. But why were these for sale? I looked around and noticed that no one in the Dhebaria Rabari community was stitching at all. Then I learned why: Stitching had been banned.

Remember, textiles are important to the Rabari, and they play a significant role in the wedding ceremony and how a married woman dresses. This collection of textiles is actually required in order for the marriage to take place. As it turns out, the Dhebaria Rabari women had been taking an extraordinarily long amount of time to finish their trousseau, purposefully creating very tiny stitches, because it meant they could delay their marriages. While this led to the creation of exquisite textiles, it was not sitting well with the overall community.

The husbands' families became upset, filing complaints with the elders who act as the governing body. They wanted their future daughters-in-law to come and live with them sooner. This began happening so regularly that the elders finally decided to ban all embroidery and appliqué. If a Rabari woman was caught stitching, she would be fined nearly $100 USD, a financially devastating amount. The elders meant business.

After asking a few more questions, I began to understand what was really happening. Historically, the Dhebaria Rebari community has had an intricately hand-stitched textile-based dowry and a bride price, namely, an amount of money that must be paid to the bride's family upon engagement. By the time the average Rabari man was able to save the requisite sum of money, he could be in his late twenties or early thirties, about ten years older than the Rabari woman he would marry. But the young Rabari women didn't want to get married to these "old" guys. Instead of lowering the bride price to a sum more easily saved, thus reducing the age gap between husbands and wives, establishing more successful engagements, and preserving the Dhebaria Rabari textiles tradition, the elders simply decided to ban the stitching altogether.

So the Dhebaria Rabari can't stitch for themselves anymore, but there is hope. In the desert there are a handful of NGOs whose sole mission is to support traditional textile legacies and to keep stitching traditions alive. The Dhebaria Rabari women have been given permission to stitch for these NGOs. And while stitching for sale is not quite the same as stitching for one's self and one's community, the younger generation *is* learning to stitch. Some NGOs are doing a really good job of teaching and allowing the Dhebaria Rabari to stitch solely in their own style, on their own pieces, instead of blending multiple

---

What is it about my own culture and upbringing that makes me want to preserve and hold? And what makes my idea or way the "right" way?

embroidery styles prevalent in the desert to create a potentially more commercially appealing product.

We all know that life changes, and with that change, it can be expected that the number of people stitching will wax and wane, too. While NGOs are providing support for the Rabari, there's one piece of the story that still bothers me. I can't wrap my head around it—and my own stash of textiles has grown as a result. Once the ban on stitching went into effect and the Rabari women stopped stitching, their textiles—stitched in the long-standing tradition that held the key to their past and reflected their identity and the way they have communicated with one another for generations—shifted in value. By which I mean these textiles were no longer of value to them. Instead, the Dhebaria Rabari women willingly sold their textiles to whoever offered enough (not much) money on any given day. How could these pieces, which have provided so many defining moments in a woman's life, be sold off? Especially in light of the fact that these textiles would never be made again?

If my family could no longer make textiles and had spent hundreds of hours in the past doing so, I would want to save them for future generations. When I asked the Rabari women why they didn't want to keep their collections, or how they felt about the ban, they didn't want to discuss it; many times their only interest in speaking to me was to try to sell me textiles and to move on.

All of these beautiful pieces were leaving the desert—this exquisite stash of work being dispersed forever. In India, it is popular for people to purchase textiles, chop them up, and stitch them together to sell to the tourist trade. I am a purist and want the textiles to stay intact. All I could think was: *Where could these textiles live?* The few local museums didn't have the desire to keep them.

But I also asked myself, as I often do when traveling and researching, *Why is this hitting me so hard?* What is it about my own culture and upbringing that makes me want to preserve and hold? And what makes my idea or way the "right" way? Why place such importance on legacy? Such focus often results in the creation of institutions that decide what and who are of value, and also the opposite, what and who are *not* of value. Can I be okay with letting things like these textiles go?

After a moment's thought, my answer was very clear: *No*. Needless to say, I could not buy every textile in the region, but I do have a small yet comprehensive collection of Dhebaria Rabari textiles. I looked for someone in the Dhebaria Rabari community who felt differently and perhaps wanted to keep a collection. I was unable to find her. But if I ever do, I have a nice stash of textiles waiting for her.

ON GIVING
BY EUGENE WYATT

In her diary, Anne Frank wrote, "No one has ever become poor by giving."

In the early 1990s, I flew to Australia and bought five world-class Saxon Merino rams to be air-freighted back to my farm in upstate New York. I became a shepherd. Today, we are proud of the wool that comes from the flock. It is Superfine Merino and has an average fiber diameter of 18 microns.

The wool is spun by Green Mountain Spinnery in Vermont, and then it is hand-dyed at my farm. On weekends, we pack up all eight weights of our Saxon Merino yarn, along with garlic, sheepskins, and our own lamb sausages, and we take it all to New York City to sell.

Friday is a busy day at the farm. We prepare for two Greenmarkets in the city that both occur on Saturday. How does one prepare for two Greenmarkets in different locations and at the same time? The answer is that Mark mans the stand in Grand Army Plaza in Brooklyn while I do the same at Union Square in Manhattan. We have two identical setups: canopies, display tables, and hundreds of colors of our hand-dyed Saxon Merino yarn. One goes in the twelve-foot trailer for me and my salespeople, the other in the ten-foot back of the market truck for Mark and his.

Saturday starts early. I tow the trailer behind the market truck from the farm to the city, where I meet Mark at 6:30 AM at the Greenmarket in Union Square. We nod a "good morning," unhook the trailer, erect the canopies, and put out some of the Saxon Merino yarn. Around 7:00, Rebecca, Sydney, and Jordan, experienced salespeople all, come to Union Square; they finish the setup and display. Then at 7:10,

Mark leaves to drive the market truck over the Manhattan Bridge to Brooklyn, where he sets up at the Greenmarket in Grand Army Plaza.

Greenmarket at Union Square on Saturday is the busiest farmers' market in New York City. It pops up and operates from 8:00 AM to 6:00 PM. It's been in the north end of Union Square for more than forty years. What makes it different from the other Greenmarkets in the city (in addition to local shoppers) is the tourists who frequent it.

Usually knitters and/or yarn browsers come into the stand before we've even got the display of yarn up. At 9:00 AM, Susan, another salesperson, comes in. She says "hello" to Rebecca, Sydney, and Jordan and helps them with the yarn display. We have bins of skeins on the back wall of the canopy, and we have hanging yarn on the side walls, all fresh from the dye pot at the farm. We greet everybody in the stand. If they say that they're just looking, we let them look. When it gets busy, Susan calls out in an unassuming voice, "If you have any yarn questions, I have yarn answers."

A red-haired woman in her late twenties looks at her questioningly. Susan smiles and, gesturing to the nearby colors, says, "Over here we have natural colors." She gestures to the other side wall: "We have what we call *citric* colors there. All the colors are dyed at the farm."

"Are the skeins priced?" the redhead asks.

"Yes, every skein is priced. It also has the weight of the skein and the yardage on the hang tag," Susan answers. "Oh, by the way, you have lovely red hair. I'm Susan, what's your name?"

"Sarah. . . . Thank you," she says with a surprised blush.

"Have a look around at the colors and the weights of yarn," Susan encourages. "Take your time; I'll be right over here skeining yarn."

Sarah looks at the yarn. She is more interested in the naturally dyed colors. She touches them, she reads the hang tags. Her thoughts are private, only they aren't quite so, because Susan is a knitter, too. She has a good idea what Sarah may be thinking.

She knows Sarah is likely saying to herself, *The yarn is so soft and*

I love that green color . . . but taking it home will just add to my stash. I have too much yarn, a closetful already. What would I do with it? I wonder if this color will go with my hair. Maybe it's not bright enough?

The green color Sarah is thinking of is a naturally dyed weld that's been overdyed with indigo to create a variegated green.

She turns to Susan. "Can you help me take it down?"

"Of course." Susan walks over to the hanging skeins, unclasps the seven-inch ring that holds several green skeins, all slightly different, and lays them on a nearby sheepskin. She leaves the ring open. Then she says, "But now you must answer a question."

Sarah looks at her inquiringly.

"Which skein would *you* like to have?" she asks. "Look at the difference between them. This one has a varied, lighter green hue to it, and this one has a more pronounced blue indigo color variation through it, and this one is a darker green . . ."

Sarah examines the skeins.

"I think . . . the lighter green one," Sarah says. "But maybe the darker . . ."

"Both will knit interestingly because of the variation in color," says Susan.

"But I should see the color against me. Do you have a mirror?" Sarah asks.

"I think so." Susan fishes in a bag that has the Catskill Merino hats in it. She finds a mirror and gives it to her.

Sarah peers at her reflection and, with the other hand, holds the green skeins against her face.

"The darker green goes well with you—it's your color," Susan declares.

Sarah nods in agreement.

"If you get one skein," Susan adds, "knit a hat. You can find a pattern on Ravelry. When it's finished, bring it on by and we'll photograph it. Or send me the photos you take. We'd love to put it up on our site, and we'll put it on Instagram!"

"Yes," agrees Sarah, "but if I add another skein to my yarn stash. . . . It's a closetful already."

"A 'closetful,' congratulations!" Susan smiles. "You're serious. A *yarn stash*, oh do I understand that. I had the same problem; I was selling my soul to the devil on MasterCard for yarn."

Sarah confesses, "I rarely shop my stash for new knitting projects. I'm too wowed by new colors of yarn. I have to have them. I buy them, but when I get home the yarn sits around, and I forget about the intended project; I usually stash it in the closet. I'm hopeless."

"You know," says Susan, "I used to go to an ashram upstate. The guru was into meditation. I'd always thought that the only way you got rid of things was either to sell them or throw them out. But the guru suggested that we *give things away*. My jaw dropped.

"I thought about it," she continues. "Yarn was very valuable to me. I was stuck between my bad habits and a growing yarn stash. So I started small at first: I gave a skein of yarn away. You know what? I felt better about myself. But it wasn't the recipient's thankfulness that made me feel better; it was the giving itself. The guru was right. That was several years ago. How I manage my stash now? I give it away."

"You give your stash away?" Sarah repeats, astonished.

"Yes, I buy yarn—my way—but without guilt or shame. When I see a color that I must have, I buy it. But I buy twice as many skeins as I need for the project. I have to feed my new addiction: giving."

"You give it away?" asks Sarah again.

"If I were you, I would buy both of the skeins—the light and the dark. Knit one and give the other away," says Susan.

"Give?" Sarah is still incredulous, but she purchases two skeins and says good-bye.

Later that day, Mark finishes at Grand Army Plaza and returns with the truck to Union Square at about 4:30 PM. We discuss how the day went in Brooklyn, how much yarn he sold, and so on. He asks me about Union Square. At 6:00 PM, he helps pack up and put things in the trailer.

Three weeks go by.

Sarah comes back to the stand. Sarah, or the knitter in her, seems to have agreed: If giving were a solution, she would do it. She'd knit the hat, she's ready for the photograph, and she says to Susan, "You know the other skein I bought? I gave it away, and it worked! It made me feel beautiful. Oh thank you, thank you, thank you."

"Congratulations! You made a lovely hat, too," Susan says with a smile. "You know what I'm proud of? You didn't stash a skein."

Sarah beams.

What you give must have value. "Estimating something as worthless," or *floccinaucinihilipilification,* is not what Sarah or Susan has in mind about yarn. To them yarn is worthwhile. To put a monetary value on it, hundreds if not thousands of dollars are in their closets or wherever they keep their yarn stashes.

Worth is what makes giving work. People don't want a gift that has no value. You must give away something that is dear to your heart, something that is worthwhile to you. Giving is a concept from ancient times. We moderns forget about the gift in this disposable age. We inhabit a sad time without generosity. How old and odd the word *charity* looks now? In the nineteenth century, when work had a similar value as a commodity, giving was alive and prevalent.

The gift not only benefits the people you give it to, but, most important, it benefits you. We are not saints, we are humans. We are transactional. We are not beyond ourselves. We gain from giving. A saint does not.

Giving is personal and small and truthful and trusty. It's like knitting.

KNITTING MY MOTHER'S STASH
BY AIMÉE OSBOURN-GILLE

When I moved to Paris in 2003, I did not have a yarn stash. I was not a knitter.

I knew the basics of knitting, having grown up with a mother who knit us everything. I always had handknit sweaters in my wardrobe. I was lucky, and I knew it. I remember being fairly young and taking an iron to a sweater, thinking I would get the kinks out of it—and being scolded gently by my mother. Instead of getting angry, she showed me what could happen. She took out what I now know is a swatch and took her iron to it; it smoked a bit, and the iron left a melted patch on the swatch. Lesson learned.

I became a knitter shortly after I moved to Paris. I was lonely. I moved to the City of Lights to be with my husband, Julien, leaving behind my life in Kansas. I started an expat blog in hopes of meeting other people like me, and I did. I made some of my best friends that first year of blogging, and guess what we did together? We knit. We started a knitting group that met every week at Starbucks. This group saved me at a time when I was feeling very lonely. Friends would join our group. We'd put bamboo needles and yarn in their hands and teach them how to knit.

I first learned to knit by watching my mother. She was always, always knitting. When I took my first pair of straight needles in my hands, they just knew what to do. I remember being about twelve years old and my mother showing me how to weave in the ends of a sweater she'd knit for my father. At the time, I was not interested in knitting, but I liked doing cross-stitch and hand-sewing. She let me weave in all her ends, and I was pleased when she said I had done it perfectly.

She told me that it's important to know how to do this or else you can ruin your handknit sweater. To this day, I love weaving in ends. It's a running joke that you can bring your ends to me at knit night, and I will weave them in for you.

I remember calling my mother from Paris and telling her that I had taken up knitting. I could tell she was smiling when she responded, "That's wonderful!"

I knew immediately that I wanted to knit a sweater for her. My LYS at the time was Le Bon Marché, my favorite department store in Paris. It is located on the Rive Gauche just a short bus ride from my apartment. At the time, I would say it was one of the best *merceries* in Paris. They carried Anny Blatt, Bouton d'Or, Rowan, Noro, Debbie Bliss, and Phildar. I had a special love for Rowan and Debbie Bliss. From time to time I would splurge on Noro, which was pretty exotic for me then. I loved Anny Blatt's pure Merino. I decided that I would knit my mother a red sweater in Debbie Bliss Baby Cashmerino. That week at knit night I cast on and started knitting the yoke. My mother called me the week after to tell me she was feeling a bit under the weather. A few days after that phone call, she passed away. I never finished the sweater. I was devastated.

I returned to Kansas for my mother's funeral. I brought the sweater I was knitting with me; I wanted to show her what I had knit. I never had the chance to knit with her, so instead I gave her my yarn and needles in hope that in the afterlife she would be able to knit with them. I could hear my mother's voice "oooh" and "ahhh" in my head when I told her the yarn was a cashmere and Merino blend. This would have been a pretty luxurious sweater for her.

I stayed in the United States for a couple of months to be close to my family. To keep myself busy I started to knit from my mother's stash. She knit with a lot of Lion Brand Thick 'n Quick and Red Heart, so I knit myself a sweater in Red Heart yarn, and I remembered my lesson on why you shouldn't iron your handknits (or at least those made with synthetics). I returned to France with two suitcases full of yarn from my mother's stash. I recognized most of it from the projects she'd worked on. She had many cotton yarns that I knew she'd planned to use for sweaters for herself. She liked to knit cotton sweaters. Her closet was full of them. Those skeins formed the beginning of my stash.

Upon my return, I found myself in a profound depression. The only thing I could do was knit. I also started to buy yarn just because. Because it was beautiful and because it made me feel something other than pain. I knit many blankets, and I would wrap myself up in them and feel like I could breathe again. I returned to my knitting group and started to dream about opening my own knit café.

By then, I'd developed a taste for beautiful luxury yarns. A friend had given me my first skein of hand-dyed yarn, SweetGeorgia, and I fell in love with the color. I searched for other such yarns, but there were very few sources in France. Blogging and Ravelry exposed me to a whole new world of knitting. I met a group of knitters in New York City who used even more amazing yarns with names like Madelinetosh and Koigu, whose twist and depth of color were very different from the classic yarns being sold in Paris. I imagined carrying these yarns in my knit café.

L'OisiveThé opened its doors in the spring of 2008. My stash began to take on epic proportions. I started buying yarn to see if I wanted to carry it in my shop. Soon yarn was showing up in every corner of our small Parisian apartment. I kept yarn stock for L'OisiveThé at our apartment, before we invested in several storage units in the neighborhood. My husband often jokes with me that the stock of L'OisiveThé takes up more real estate in Paris than we do. I refer to the stock of L'OisiveThé, and that of our new shop, La Bien Aimée, as my yarn stash. I have knitted with every yarn we carry and love them all very much. I take so much pleasure when someone walks into my shop and finds their happiness in yarn. It is the most satisfying feeling to know you have the perfect match for the project they envision.

I have a very European view of how knitters stash, as I have never really shopped for yarn, knit, or stashed in the United States. All my customers are unique in their knitting styles. My local customers aren't always the most intrepid of knitters. I am not talking about my expatriate knitters but the true locals who live on the street of L'OisiveThé or in the neighborhood surrounding La Bien Aimée. I feel good if I can get them to buy one skein to try out—and I have a very long list of one-skein projects in my Ravelry page to entice them. I am happy to say that my local clientele is gradually becoming the intrepid community of knitters I dreamed they would be. I love it when they return to the shop, so pleased with their yarn choices and ready to buy more. These knitters are what I call the "buy and knit" knitters. They don't buy unless they know exactly what they are going to make.

Being an American who owns two yarn shops in Paris, I also attract a lot of knitters passing through town on their holidays or business travels. I'm always humbled when people tell me that they put L'OisiveThé or La Bien Aimée on their list of things to do after seeing places like the Eiffel Tower or the Louvre. These knitters are on a mission. They want what they can't get at home, and they are willing to buy to expand their stash. I love to ask, "What will you make with your selection today?" The majority say they don't know; it's just pretty and they have to have it.

If you've ever attended knit night or spent an afternoon at L'OisiveThé, you've had a glimpse of the different kinds of knitters who come through our doors. I have a client who buys only blue yarn, for example. Blue is her favorite color. Look at her stash on Ravelry and you'll see it's all different shades of blue. She told me once that her husband bought her a new house with an extra room specifically to stash her blue yarn. Another loyal client of mine lives in what we call a "cozy" Paris apartment, yet she has the most impressive stash. She is a librarian, and you'd better believe that everything is perfectly cataloged. She makes the most of her high ceilings with custom floor-to-ceiling shelves to arrange her stash (by color and project).

I had another client tell me that she has never stashed yarn in her life. She buys yarn only when she is ready and has a project picked out. A very prolific knitter, she is constantly producing something amazing. But recently she came into La Bien Aimée to say hello. She bought a sweater's quantity of La Bien Aimée house-brand yarn in her favorite colors. Knowing her knitting habits, I asked her which pattern she was going to knit. She looked me straight in the eye, a bit scared and a bit excited, and said she didn't have a project in mind. She saw these beautiful colors and had to have them. She made sure to buy enough just in case she wanted to make a sweater.

I have been a knitter for more than fourteen years now, and I've noticed that my stash habits have evolved. I want to produce more and buy less. I've stopped buying yarn "just because" and have started shopping for yarn based on the project. It feels more manageable to buy yarn in this way. Most of my yarn is cataloged and sitting in a storage unit—except for my mother's yarn stash. It lives in my bedroom, and I look through it often.

The other day I was showing my daughter, Alixe, her grand-mother's yarn. She pulled out each skein to inspect. She put most skeins aside, as she was not interested in them. But she found some wool-blend bouclé and hugged it, saying how soft it was. She rubbed it against her face like she does with her favorite *doudou*, and then I knew. It has been ten years since I inherited my mother's stash, and I've never knit anything from it except the Red Heart sweater. But after seeing my daughter fondle that bouclé yarn so lovingly, it brought me so much joy that a project was born in that moment. I wound it up, because the time has come for me to knit my mother's stash.

MARK OF THE HAND, MARK ON THE HEART
BY KIM MCBRIEN EVANS

I live in a house that often feels as if it's made of yarn. As a yarn dyer, for the last seven years my home has been, for all intents and purposes, a yarn shop. With in-house dyers. Where, if what I need immediately is not at hand, I can make it.

My life has been this way ever since I cast on my first potholder at age four. It was pink. And acrylic. Even then, working with colors and materials I hated, the simple act of creating stitch after stitch, imagining a life for this potholder and how it would be used, was enough to drown out the mocking sounds of my kindergarten nemesis, Joey Coffee.

That early memory was my first clue that I was hooked on the power of being able to make things with my hands—and that those things are intrinsically connected to the people who make them.

In my studio, I have a cupboard labeled "Lickedenstein" where yarns that I just can't part with live until I know what they need to be. There is a certain freedom and sense of satisfaction in being able to knit with yarn you've created yourself—to make exactly what you need and want to work with, to know those stories and memories and inspirations so intimately, to wrap your hands in that warmth. But this yarn, my work yarn, is not my stash.

I do have a stash. An important one, because it doesn't represent the pressure of unrealized projects or impending gifts. Important, because it's never mattered how much space it takes up, even when my space was a four-hundred-and-fifty-square-foot city apartment. I don't care how quickly I use it up, how long that hand-dyed skein of Corriedale from that farm in Nova Scotia has lived in it, or whether I

*My stash has no deadlines and no expectations.
Just memories and history. I simply care about
the people and places it represents.*

ever use it at all. My stash has no deadlines and no expectations. Just memories and history. I simply care about the people and places it represents.

No single thing in my house is valued more than those things made by hand. Every member of my family, as far back as any of us can remember, has done some kind of handwork. Grandad told stories about sitting around the kitchen table with his brothers and knitting washcloths for the war effort. My mother threw her needlepoint at my fidgety father and told him to finish it, launching his lifetime love affair with color and stitches. I dug through deep baskets of fluff with my mother and learned how spin with a drop spindle in the basement of a yarn shop in Toronto that still stands. My rebellious younger brother looked up from hand-sewing patches on his jacket and, to his amusement, realized he was one of us. It's no mistake that the greatest expression of love from anyone in my family is something handmade.

Summers were spent traveling from one artist's studio to another, watching them create in their own unique environment. Every time I use one of the pieces gathered during that time, it's a visit with that person. The conversations we've had. Meeting the eyes of goats that grew fiber that became woven cloth. The light in a woodworker's eyes as she told me that the magic secret of fine charcoal-gray lines was the result of burying the wood in the forest for the winter. Each maker leaves a mark through his or work. Pick up a handmade object, and you can read its maker's stories with your fingers.

Makers of all kinds don't just "make" things. They infuse the objects with their state of mind and mood, with their experience and skill. Yarn is no different. Whether it's handspun or hand-dyed, once the maker's hand has touched the yarn, it's no longer just yarn. It is infused with everything that maker does and is. My stash overflows with these kinds of skeins.

Beside my front door is a set of coat hooks made from three antique spoons found within a piece of an old weathered barn down the road. Three long creamy skeins hang on these hooks. Undyed, they represent the journey from sheep to shearer, farmer to processing, mill to my door. These skeins tell the story of love for every level of this work we do, and for the animals that produce beautiful fiber for us. I look at these skeins every day. I touch them as I walk past, letting the strands fall through my fingers. I know these sheep—their sounds, their smells still present in the fiber. I know the people who spin these yarns, and the long history of their craft and their mills. I love knowing each step of the journey these skeins have taken to my door.

You cannot be any kind of textile artist and not be aware of—and constantly try to refine—each step of what you do. A few years ago I spent a week with textile artist India Flint. She showed me a new way of looking at the physical world around me and imprinting that world on my stash. I've started traveling with a small dye pot. I gather leaves and plants and bark and sticks, chunks of rusty metal and copper wire found in the street—all bits and pieces of the place I'm in. I find a yarn shop or farmers' market, buy undyed yarn from that region, which already has much to tell me, and then I let the plants and fiber work together. I wrap the yarn and plantstuff in layers and wait, not so patiently, for it to cook and cool and be unwrapped. What I'm left with is yarn from a place that is marked by pieces of that place. It's usually imperfect and definitely not repeatable—the ultimate souvenir of where I've traveled.

Nowhere in yarndom is the mark of the hand more evident than in a hand-dyer's studio. We are all different. Given the same dye recipe, following the same technique, and even standing side by side, yarn from three different dyers will be different. Even skeins in the same pot will be unique. The mark of the hand is impossible to replace. It reveals the world as seen through the yarn-dyer's eyes.

I'm most attracted to yarn that's been dyed in ways that make me see color differently or challenge my perception of what "goes together." The mark of the hand is present in these skeins. Hand-dyers are never in competition with each other. Rather, we push each other to expand our worlds.

One of my favorite rings was made from a one-foot length of silver, simply hammered and wrapped around my finger—a single piece of metal, so simple, but every part of it shows the mark of the maker. That mark is something that only I, as the wearer, see. Nestled on a small shelf is a bundle of ruby-red Merino that has the same intimate effect on me. Holding one skein in my hands, I see quiet shifts and layers of color not visible from a distance, appearing only as subtle texture. But the depth that passes through my fingers with each stitch is a conversation, much like the ones I'd have with the dyer herself.

Nothing we ever do is entirely on our own. We are creative collaborators—designer and dyer, teacher and student, a balance of minds and hands that can create immense beauty. At our studio Dye Camp, I see this reflected in my students, who stretch their new creative muscles. First-timers learn the basics and try everything with caution. Returning students gain more confidence, break more rules, and become wildly creative, each in his or her own way.

The yarns that result are spectacular and occupy a special place in my stash. I have a particular weakness for the cakes of yarn I've seen grow from a *What would happen if* . . . hypothesis into breathtakingly beautiful gradients. What about that person who is just starting to learn? Holding a skein of muted stone shades, I may see fear, anxiety, disappointment, and frustration at hands that produced something other than what the mind envisioned. But I get to watch those feelings change over the course of a few days or even a few hours. This skein

Makers of all kinds don't just "make" things. They infuse the objects with their state of mind and mood, with their experience and skill. Yarn is no different. Whether it's handspun or hand-dyed, once the maker's hand has touched the yarn, it's no longer just yarn. It is infused with everything that maker does and is. My stash overflows with these kinds of skeins.

is about learning. It's about expectations and realizing that it's okay to love something that turned out different than you planned. These seven skeins of watery blues over here tell me about striving for the best you can be. I turn them over with deep care, thinking about who they are for and what they represent.

Yarn is a finished object with a story that never ends. It was sheep or silk or plant. It became string. It developed color through dyeing or the quiet aging that all natural things go through. It has passed from hand to hand. It might become more. It might always be a memory or an idea. But every single skein in my stash makes me happy. It has a memory attached to it. The yarn reminds me of people who are too far away, and it brings them closer to me. If it does all that, it belongs in the comfort of my stash.

STASH BYPASS
BY ADRIENNE MARTINI

My mom was never a knitter.

I have some vague memory of her trying to learn, once upon a time, but it just wasn't her jam. Mom did crochet, though. To be more specific, Mom was a double crocheter and would churn out blanket after blanket with row on top of row of double crochet. Whenever I was feeling puckish, I'd offer to teach her the triple crochet, just to shake things up. But no. Her hands knew double crochet, and it was a comfort.

The same was true of good old Red Heart Yarn, which she'd buy two or three skeins of at a time. If those ran out before any given blanket was done, she'd pick up another skein or two at one of the nearby "marts," either Wal- or K-. Frequently, those new skeins would only vaguely be related to the colors she'd already crocheted. Yards of soft pink would abruptly become one skein's worth of dark brown and yellow variegated, which would finish up with one row of green. The next blanket would then start with that same green. It wasn't so much that she was crocheting many blankets; she was crocheting a really big one that kept getting interrupted. Those blankets should have come with a trigger warning for those who like order. It's not as if there are real dye lots when it comes to Red Heart. You can buy the exact same color in any store anywhere at any time. That industrial color control is Red Heart's main selling point. True, it's also cheap—so cheap that you could easily buy enough for an entire blanket with a $20 bill and still have enough left over for a snack. But that's not the way my mom operated. That kind of thinking requires commitment and minimal planning, which she prefers to leave to other people, particularly those people to whom she gave birth and who are innately anal-retentive.

I am so anal-retentive, in fact, that the admissions person at Mom's hastily arranged assisted living center complimented me on my ability to fill out paperwork, which is a thing I love to do anyway because capturing life's messes on boilerplate forms makes me feel like I can pin it down enough to understand it. I like my stash, both literal and metaphorical, to be understandable.

My actual yarn stash fits in five medium plastic bins under a queen-size bed. Mostly, it's yarn that functions as an *aide mémoire*—you know, just one hank of hand-dyed silk from that amazing store in London or those delicious balls of angora your best friend gave you that once belonged to her mother, and the vials of glass beads from Prague that will be perfect knitted into a scarf, maybe from that silk. Of course, there's some workhorse Regia sock yarn, which I buy when I stumble across the ones designed by Kaffe Fassett. I also have another whole tote dedicated to balls of Noro Kuyeon, which I always buy when I find it on sale, even though I have no practical plans for it.

I keep any yarn that has been acquired for a concrete project in the linen closet and frequently print off a copy of the pattern to store with it. As I type, there are two waiting for their turn on the needles. It's a system that works for me. I do love a good system. But systems break down.

I briefly thought about pulling a ball of Regia and some needles out of the stash for the trip to tiny Lee, Florida, where my mom has lived for the last decade. My current projects were too cumbersome for travel knitting, and I'd need to cast on something more appropriate for planes (no trains) and automobiles. At the time, it seemed like too much work. It was a thousand times less complicated to grab an unread issue of *Real Simple* and a book I'd been trying to finish.

Besides, I wasn't planning to be away for very long. I flew down from Albany, New York, after work on a Monday; drove ninety minutes from Jacksonville in the pitch black in a monsoon; and got to Mom's by 11:00 PM. We were up at 4:00 AM to make the forty-five-minute drive up to Valdosta, Georgia, where she'd have a heart catheterization and, likely, a stent or two placed. I'd get her back home, settled, and then fly back the next afternoon.

But that's not what happened. The heart procedure was over almost before it started, when the doc did his first look-see and realized that she had enough occlusions to warrant a quintuple bypass, which was one more bypass than I thought was possible. We have always been a family that goes that extra mile.

Then, there were hospital rooms and waiting rooms and waiting in hospital rooms. There were scrambles to rearrange flights and cars and hotel rooms and rides for my kids back home. There was a quick trip back to my mom's house to grab my stuff, so that I could stay up in Valdosta for the duration. There were many moments of feeling completely helpless.

To see me through it all, there was no knitting. None. Because grabbing that ball of yarn that I already had under my bed was apparently too much of a bother. Shortly after mom went into the OR, I spotted a woman in the cavernous hospital lobby knitting away on a scarf. I sat as close as I could to her without making it weird. Maybe she'd let me do just one little row? Maybe if I asked nicely and assured her that I wasn't a complete nut, just a knitter separated from her stash? Maybe, I thought, I should pull it together, consult the Google oracle, and go look for my own dang yarn even though I have plenty at home. Then that thought was gone, replaced by staring off into the middle distance and quietly weeping, because the word *home* reminded me how uncertain the near future was.

For the record, I don't know when my mother stopped crocheting afghans. For decades, we've lived at least a thousand miles apart, which made dropping in to check on her crocheting something that never happened. The physical distance was only part of the reason why.

Days later, I flew back to my own stash. Saying good-bye to my mom, who remained in rough shape after surgery but was out of immediate danger, was wrenching. I had the advantage of knowing she was in better hands than mine. Her main caregiver, in fact, wanted to hug me as I was walking my sobbing self out the door but held back because, as she said, "I know Yankees aren't big huggers." And, yes, she correctly read this particular Yankee.

I was back on a plane a few weeks later to settle her into an assisted-living facility near Orlando. I had the beginnings of a sock by this time, which I'd cast on shortly after getting home, but still the knitting didn't come with me, because I had other goals for the trip that would get in the way of real knitting time. I needed to plan how to pack up and sell her house because it wasn't going to be her house anymore. And that is a much longer story that has zero to do with yarn, other than the fact that I did get an alarming amount of knitting done at home while talking on the phone to various agencies and relatives.

The three-hour drive to Lee from Central Florida should have been enough time to prepare myself for what I found when I walked into my mom's house. Everything was just as we'd left it. That shouldn't have been a surprise, really, but so much else had changed that this should have, too. Those slices of red velvet cake that were to be a treat after the procedure were still in the fridge. The gifts I was supposed to take back to her grandchildren were still in the middle of the dining room table. The mess I'd made while rummaging through the house when I decamped for Georgia. Where do you even start?

I started by sitting in my mom's recliner and closing my eyes . . . and opening them again, because ignoring what I don't want to deal with helped create this situation in the first place.

Right in my line of sight on the corner of the fireplace hearth was a basket of yarn.

I know that seems far too poetic to be true. And, yet, here we are. Me looking at a small basket of yarn in the house of a woman who doesn't stash yarn. Its origin story remains a mystery for reasons far too depressing to go into.

It wasn't full of Red Heart, her yarn of choice. Instead it was full of interesting yarns you'd need to seek out, like Rowan and Manos del Uruguay. On the top of the pile was a single skein of Jamieson & Smith, a yarn I have an affinity for, in a light lavender just a smidge darker than the one I'd painted on my walls in junior high.

Most of the yarn went into the donation pile, where it can delight knitters and crocheters unknown to me. But that one skein made the long trip back with me. It's in the stash now, next to the angora, the silk, and the beads. Waiting.

A STASH OF ONE'S OWN: YARN AS A FEMINIST ISSUE
BY DEBBIE STOLLER

When I first got into knitting, in the late nineties, I quickly realized that there was an entire alphabet soup of abbreviations and acronyms I would need to learn, such as *ssk* and *k2tog*, in order to become proficient in this craft. But as I began to spend time on knitting blogs and message boards, I saw there were quite a few more I'd need to familiarize myself with as well, such as *WIP*, *UFO*, *KIP*, and *LYS*. There was one, however, that baffled me for quite a while before I figured it out: *DH*. Eventually I came to understand that *DH* meant "Dear Husband," and I noticed that the acronym appeared in two main conversation topics. The first, of course, was when folks would talk about the things that they were making for DH, including socks, hats, and huge sweaters. But almost as often, DH would come up in conversations about people's yarn stashes. Many knitters, it seemed, were concerned about hiding theirs from their DH.

I have never had a DH, although I have had an LTB (long-term boyfriend) for the past two decades. My LTB, however, is not an LIB (live-in boyfriend). Also, I am not FD (financially dependent) on my DLTB. As a result, we have never had a conversation about my yarn stash, and I have never given any thought to hiding it from him.

So perhaps I'm the last person on earth who should be weighing in on what all this hiding-the-yarn-stash-from-DH kerfuffle is all about. Yet as both a feminist and an *I Love Lucy* fan, I feel I must. Because the first image that comes to mind whenever I read about a knitter admitting that she has just purchased new skeins of yarn that she must hide before "DH finds out" is that fabulous redhead. I'm thinking of those episodes of the classic TV show where Lucy would have bought something—usually a new hat (I'm guessing hats were sort of the shoes of the fifties? Because really, even as a knitter, who needs so many hats?)—and would have to find a way to hide it from Ricky. He had either told her at the beginning of the episode that she already had too many hats, or that she had to stick to her monthly household budget or she'd have loads of 'splainin' to do. But Lucy, she just couldn't help herself. She'd see the perfect hat, and she'd buy it, and then she'd have to find a place to hide it before Ricky got home. Hilarity would ensue. And sometimes, at the end, Lucy would be taken over Ricky's knee and spanked. Because that was a totally fine thing to do in the fifties. At least on *I Love Lucy* it was.

Watching Lucy in reruns as a child in the seventies was one of many things that primed me to become a feminist when I grew up. Even at age ten it was obvious to me that women had the deck stacked against them. For one thing, there were few opportunities for work outside the home (aside from, say, a job at a chocolate factory). For another, even when they worked hard to keep up their side of the bargain—keeping the home clean, doing the laundry and the cooking and the childrearing—they still weren't entitled to an equal say in the family's finances.

So as much as I loved Lucy, I knew I didn't want a life like hers. I wanted a future where women and men were equal partners; where even if one of them was the primary wage earner, the money would belong to both of them equally. I didn't want to grow up in a world where a husband was more like a parent than a partner: doling out an allowance and punishing you when you were naughty.

But once I was an adult and living in that future, what was I to make of women on these knitting message boards who still seemed to be trapped in some modern-day Lucy-Ricky-hat scenario? Giving it some thought, I came to the conclusion that there were really only three reasons that someone would need to hide their yarn collection from their life partner. The first would be that they are planning to make something with that yarn for said partner, and they want it to be a surprise. But in that case, there would be only a small amount of yarn that would need to be hidden; certainly one's entire stash wouldn't be devoted to creating things only for the man of the house?

Another reason to hide one's stash, I suppose, is because one's DH is usually also a roommate or housemate, and the space has to be shared fairly. And if someone's yarn stash is getting so out of control that they are taking over more than their fair share of storage space, then yes, they may not want to disclose to their DH that they just bought an additional garbage-bag-full of closeout yarn. But if this is the case, then they'd want to keep it from their DD (daughter) and DS (son) as well, or anyone else sharing a roof with them and their abundance of yarn. And if one's yarn stash is beginning to overtake their living space, then they just might be a hoarder. They certainly shouldn't hide this fact from their DH (although he probably already knows). Instead, they need to get help, lest they end up sleeping on a bed covered so high in yarn balls they need to use a ladder just to get into it.

On the other hand, perhaps they don't want their DH to see the yarn they've got stored away because then he would know how much money they've spent, and continue to spend, on this hobby of theirs. Again, I don't know how different couples decide to work out their finances, but here there should certainly be no secrets. And if they think he'd be upset because really, the two of them are strapped for cash and the roof needs fixing and they can barely buy enough baby and cat food to keep all their dependents in delicious mush, then they've got no business buying yarn at all (especially if they already have a yarn stash!). I mean, what kind of a person would want to share this type of fiscally irresponsible behavior in an online message board such as one on Ravelry titled "Flash Your Stash," with a picture of their living room furniture entirely covered in yarn balls and a note saying that the photo could only be taken when "DH was out of the house"? These folks also might need to get help—unless they plan on fixing that holey roof with yarn balls (it would felt, I guess, but I wouldn't recommend it).

No; while each of these are reasons women often give for why they are secretive about their stash, I think there is another reason that they frequently feel compelled to hide their yarn from their DH, and it actually has very little to do with their DH at all. I think many women are uncomfortable about having a large collection of balls and skeins and hanks because it runs counter to what is expected of them as women.

That's because a yarn stash makes a pretty large statement to the world that a woman is planning to spend hours—nay, years—of her life engaging in something that doesn't promise to make her skinnier or look younger or give her a tighter butt. Something that won't make her a better mother, or a better wife. That she is dedicated to finding time now, and for the foreseeable future, to do something that, unlike cooking, doesn't really benefit anyone but herself (okay, yes, we make things for other people but, c'mon: We knit because we enjoy it). It announces to the world that she has decided to do something just for herself, in the pursuit of only one thing: pleasure.

A yarn stash takes up a lot of room, too. Yarn balls are quite a bit larger than spools of thread or embroidery floss or even books. Developing a yarn stash requires a commitment of space that many other hobby supplies don't command, and, in almost all circumstances, women are expected to take up as little space as possible. And in much the same way that Virginia Woolf once argued that, if women were to become successful writers, they needed money and "a room of one's own," accumulating a yarn stash means that one has succeeded not just in literally securing a room of your own—the space a stash requires—but also that a woman has figuratively made room in her life for this hobby, this craft, this form of meditation, from which she gets so much enjoyment.

All of this runs counter to what society expects from women.

*That's because a yarn stash makes a
pretty large statement to the world that a
woman is planning to spend hours—nay,
years—of her life engaging in something
that doesn't promise to make her skinnier
or look younger or give her a tighter butt.*

We are certainly not encouraged to indulge in anything for the mere sake of pleasure—except for a small piece of chocolate once a week, or maybe a bubble bath. I mean, how many times have you seen a women's magazine or website propose a "weekend of indulgence" that includes baths, face masks, and possibly a pedicure? These seem to be some of the few acceptable ways that we women are allowed to "treat" ourselves. But when I think of an indulgent weekend, I think of having pizza for breakfast, lunch, and dinner; I think of staying out all night drinking whiskey and flirting with younger men; I think of spending an entire day in my pajamas knitting and watching documentaries on Netflix—I certainly don't think of a *bath*. In fact, taking care that one is clean and pore-free and has her talons in tip-top form isn't an indulgence for women—it is an imperative. There's no indulgence in doing what one's already expected to do.

Now, I know that no women's magazine is ever going to encourage women to indulge themselves by buying more yarn. But they've got it all wrong. Because every time a person buys yarn for a future project they are going to make "someday," they are reaffirming their commitment to spend many delicious hours doing something they love. A woman's growing stash is a monument to her never-ending, happily-ever-after love affair with yarn; to the ongoing respect for her craft; and to the value of doing something just for herself.

And none of these are things women should be ashamed of, or feel guilty about, or laugh off with an embarrassed shrug. And they certainly aren't anything one should be hiding from the human with whom they have decided to share a life.

Because the way I see it, it's sexism, pure and simple, that makes a woman feel ashamed of her yarn stash, while her husband, who has enough parts in the garage to make five motorcycles, doesn't display the slightest bit of embarrassment about it. It's sexism that makes a woman believe that an investment in hundreds of dollars of skin creams promising to restore her youth is an acceptable expenditure, when the same amount spent on yarn is considered to have been squandered, because our culture expects women to be forever young. It's sexism that makes hobbies engaged in mostly by women, such as knitting, considered frivolous wastes of time, while those engaged in mostly by men, such as fishing or golf, are never judged as harshly.

So I say to women: Flaunt your stash. Own it. Find a way to share your space and your finances with your DH that seems fair and equal, because no modern partnership should be based on anything less. Then fill that closet, or those shelves, or that craft room, or that suitcase, with as much yarn as you can fit and afford.

Stake your place in the world inside a circle of yarn balls. Stand up for your right to life, liberty, and the pursuit of a yarn stash. It's your duty as a knitter, and as a woman.

ABOUT THE CONTRIBUTORS

SUSAN B. ANDERSON lives, knits, and designs in Madison, Wisconsin. In 2016, Susan proudly launched Barrett Wool Co., her new 100-percent American wool yarn and pattern line found at BarrettWoolCo.com. Susan has authored six knitting books, including the popular *Itty-Bitty Hats*, *Itty-Bitty Nursery*, *Itty-Bitty Toys*, *Topsy-Turvy Inside-Out*, and *Kids' Knitting Workshop* (all Artisan). Susan has three popular Craftsy workshops. For the past ten years, she has written her award-winning blog, found at SusanBAnderson.blogspot.com. Susan designs for her self-published pattern line and has had designs in *Parents Magazine*, *Knit Simple*, *Interweave Knits*, and *Noro Magazine*, as well as a printed pattern line with Alana Dakos's NNK Press. Susan's favorite part of her career is being a knitting teacher. She loves traveling the country teaching and meeting knitters from all over the world.

RACHEL ATKINSON is a yarn purveyor (Daughter of a Shepherd) and the real-life daughter of a shepherd. Wool is truly in her blood. She is a knitting and crochet designer and technical editor with dreams of owning her own flock of sheep and building a library in which to catalog both her paper ephemera and stash. You can find her at DaughterofaShepherd.com.

AMY CHRISTOFFERS is the Design Director at Berroco, the designer of Savory Knitting patterns, and the author of the book *New American Knits* (Interweave). She divides her time between Rhode Island, where she works, and Vermont, where she escapes to a tiny house in the mountains that's stuffed with yarn and books.

KAY GARDINER has a lifelong ability to turn things she enjoys doing anyway into her job for real. Argumentative from infancy, she went to law school and subsequently worked as a trial lawyer for seventeen years, including a dozen years as an Assistant United States Attorney for the Southern District of New York. In her thirties, she took up knitting, which she had learned in childhood as a Camp Fire Girl, and it slowly took over her life. Kay "met" Ann Shayne on the Rowan Yarns chat board in the early 2000s. Together they started a blog, *Mason-Dixon Knitting*, which became a central part of their lives and a real place in their minds. Together they wrote two knitting books, *Mason-Dixon Knitting* and *Mason-Dixon Knitting Outside the Lines* (both Potter Craft). They continued to write about knitting while life happened, their children grew, and their stoic friends and families accepted that the knitting thing was not going away. In 2016, Ann and Kay went all in and renovated MasonDixonKnitting.com into a daily online magazine featuring articles, humor, and inspiration from as many sources of fun as possible, and of course a shop crammed full of the knitterly things they love most at any given moment. Kay has a teenage daughter and son and a bad-tempered terrier, all of whom model knitwear at low, low rates.

LILITH GREEN is *the* Old Maiden Aunt, yarn-dyer extraordinaire, and Queen of Everything (at least at the OMA studio). After a circuitous path through various forms of education and employment, encompassing a degree in English Literature, waitressing, office/admin work, and training as a violin maker, she finally found her niche/obsession in the world of knitting, spinning, and dyeing. She lives in the village of West Kilbride on the west coast of Scotland, and you can find her at OldMaidenAunt.com.

FRANKLIN HABIT is the author of *It Itches: A Stash of Knitting Cartoons* (Interweave) and *I Dream of Yarn: A Knit and Crochet Color-*

ing Book (Sixth & Spring). His writing and designs have appeared in *Vogue Knitting, Interweave Knits, Interweave Crochet, PieceWork, PLY, Knitty,* and *Twist Collective.* He contributes monthly to the Lion Brand Yarns Notebook and Mason-Dixon Knitting, and produces his popular "Fridays with Franklin" columns for Skacel Collection/ Makers' Mercantile. Many of his independently published patterns are available via Ravelry. He lives in Chicago with 15,000 books, two spinning wheels, three looms, and a yarn stash that fits under the bed. (It's a very big bed.)

RACHAEL HERRON is the bestselling author of more than fifteen novels, including the Cypress Hollow knit-lit series and the memoir *A Life in Stitches* (Chronicle). She received her MFA in writing from Mills College in Oakland, and she teaches writing in the extension programs at both UC Berkeley and Stanford. She has a lot of comfort stash (just in case) and very little other stash. She refuses to divulge how much pre-yarn fiber she has, though. You'll find her at RachaelHerron.com.

AMY HERZOG loves helping knitters create garments they love to wear. She's the creator of the CustomFit pattern generator and the author of *Knit to Flatter, Knit Wear Love,* and *You Can Knit That* (all Abrams). She teaches across the country and on Craftsy, and her designs have been published in *Rowan Magazine, Interweave Knits,* and more. She lives in Connecticut with her husband, two boys, two cats, and the button stash she collects instead of yarn. Find out more at AmyHerzogDesigns.com.

GUDRUN JOHNSTON was born at home in a wee village within spitting distance of the sea in Shetland. She was immediately swathed in hap shawls, which apparently made a lasting impression. She's the owner of the Shetland Trader line of knitwear designs—which marks the second life of a company first started by her mother in the seventies. She's inordinately proud that her stash includes knitwear items, photos, and paraphernalia to remind her of her home and heritage. You'll find her at TheShetlandTrader.com.

ANNA MALTZ houses her stash in London, though she can often be found teaching knitting all over the world. An avid sweaterspotter and knit detective who sees the world through yarn-tinted spectacles, she writes knitting patterns and a regular column for *Pom Pom Quarterly*. You'll find her at AnnaMaltz.com and on Instagram as @sweaterspotter.

ADRIENNE MARTINI is a writer, runner, knitter, and mother living in New York State. She has written two memoirs—one about knitting, one about mothers—for Simon & Schuster, and she is a regular fixture at AnotherMotherRunner.com and Mason-Dixon Knitting. Pictures of Adrienne's corgi, Lucy, have threatened to break the Internet. Her stash is small and mostly fits under a queen-size bed.

KIM MCBRIEN EVANS knit her way to a BFA in classical music—her first clue that she was a lifelong textile maven and there was no stopping that. After many years wrangling professional divas, artists, and an arts council or two, she fled the art rat race and conjured up the circus that is Indigodragonfly. Now she lives in the middle of the Canadian woods and produces hand-dyed yarn known for deep, multifaceted colors and clever, offbeat names. She spends most days elbow-deep in yarn and color and teaching others how to bend these to their will. Follow her yarns and blog at Indigodragonfly.ca.

JILLIAN MORENO, author of *Yarnitecture: A Knitter's Guide to Spinning: Building Exactly the Yarn You Want* (Storey), can't stop writing and teaching about spinning and using handspun to knit, weave, and stitch. She explores, questions, and plays, and she wants to take as many people as possible along for the ride. She enthusiastically encourages her students and readers to feel confidence and joy making and using their handspun, even if it means singing and dancing in class. If you can't find her teaching in person you can find her on Craftsy and in *Knittyspin*, *PLY Magazine*, and *Spin-Off Magazine*. When she's at home in Ann Arbor, Michigan, she can be found wantonly basking in her stash. Keep up with her fiber exploits at JillianMoreno.com.

LELA NARGI has written several books and numerous articles about the art, craft, and history of knitting from her home in Brooklyn, New York. Her stash, such as it is, consists of bittersweet leftovers from all the sweaters she's ever knit for her newly teenage daughter—who now regularly raids it for her own dastardly knitting purposes. You'll find her at LelaNargi.com.

AIMÉE OSBOURN-GILLE is the owner of L'OisiveThé, a tea house and yarn shop, and La Bien Aimée, a yarn shop and dye studio, both located in Paris, France. You will always find a pair of knitting needles in her hands and yarn in her bag. Her tiny Parisian apartment is overflowing with yarn. Aimée's children and husband find it perfectly normal to find yarn in their sock drawers and under their beds. Aimée has been knitting (and stashing yarn) since 2003. Online at LOisiveThe.com and LaBienAimee.com.

STEPHANIE PEARL-MCPHEE is the *New York Times*–bestselling author of eight humorous books, seven of which have a lot to do with knitting. She's been knitting for more than forty years and is also the author of the popular and long-lived blog *Yarn Harlot* and part of the magic at the Strung Along Retreats for knitters. Stephanie loves to talk about knitting and thinks that most people would be surprised how important she thinks it is. She's the mother of three, wife of one, can drive a standard, and has owned two cats in a row that don't care much for her. Stephanie lives in an untidy, wool-filled house in Toronto, Canada. She writes at YarnHarlot.com.

SUE SHANKLE is a licensed clinical social worker who lives with her canine family in Greensboro, North Carolina. She considers herself a yarn collector.

ANN SHAYNE likes anything having to do with writing, editing, knitting, and trying to make the world more cheerful. She has worked in New York in book publishing; edited *BookPage*, a book-review publication; published *Bowling Avenue*, a novel; and served on a number of nonprofit boards in her beloved home, Nashville. In 2003, she and her longtime knitting co-conspirator, Kay Gardiner, began *Mason-Dixon Knitting*, a blog that led them to publish two books, *Mason-Dixon Knitting* and *Mason-Dixon Knitting Outside the Lines* (both Potter Craft). In October 2016, Mason-Dixon Knitting became a wide-ranging new website that is a destination for knitters in search of inspiration, community, great writers, beautiful patterns, and special yarns. And swag with a swirly little MDK logo on it. There's always something new at Mason-Dixon Knitting, she is quick to say, mostly because she and Kay can type one hundred words a minute. Ann's husband, Jon, is remarkably supportive, and her two sons are patient, if long suffering.

DEBBIE STOLLER is the author of the *New York Times*–bestselling *Stitch 'n Bitch* knitting and crocheting books (Storey). She is also the co-publisher and editor in chief of the feminist magazine *BUST* (Bust.com). She holds a PhD in the Psychology of Women from Yale, and her secret superpower is that she is bilingual in Dutch and English. Debbie shares her Brooklyn dream house with three crazy dogs, one nutsy cat, and way too much yarn.

MEG SWANSEN is a knitting designer, publisher, author, and teacher. She cofounded and owns a knitting supply and publishing business, Schoolhouse Press, and she heads up four consecutive weeks of her annual summer Knitting Camp—founded by her mother, Elizabeth Zimmermann, in 1974. Meg lives and works in an old Wisconsin schoolhouse, surrounded by her stash of wool, books, and helpful cats. Her work, and a link to her blog, can be found at SchoolhousePress.com.

KRISTINE VEJAR started her first stash—consisting of pink calico cotton fabrics—when she was six years old. Today, her stash spans five rooms—one of which is a seventeen-hundred-square-foot store named A Verb for Keeping Warm, located in Oakland, California. Kristine's love of textiles has taken her around the world and led to her discovery of natural dyeing, her current favorite practice. She is the author of *The Modern Natural Dyer* (Abrams). You'll find her at AVerbforKeepingWarm.com.

EUGENE WYATT is a shepherd. His words and yarn can be found at Catskill-Merino.com.